LINGERIE & BEACHWEAR

LINGERIE & BEACHWEAR
1,000 FASHION DESIGNS

DORINA CROCI

**With the collaboration
of Elisabetta Drudi**

PROMOPRESS 11

To my dearest mum for having given me,
as well as sound principles,
imagination and creativity,
together with the pursuit of style and elegance.

Hoaki Books, S.L.
C/ Ausiàs March, 128
08013 Barcelona, Spain
T. 0034 935 952 283
F. 0034 932 654 883
info@hoakibooks.com
www.hoaki.com

Lingerie & Beachwear
1,000 Fashion Designs

ISBN: 978-84-17412-52-4
D.L.: B 14079-2019
Printed in China

Copyright © 2019 Hoaki
Copyright © 2019 Ikon Editrice srl
Original title: Lingerie & Beachwear

English translation: Mariotti Translations
Illustrations: Elisabetta Drudi
Model review: Maristella Olivoto
Layout and editing: Martina Panarello, Wendy Moreira

Contents

Lingerie

The world of Lingerie encompasses a wide variety of underwear. It includes nightgowns, pyjamas, dressing gowns or house robes, slips, vests, as well as the entire range of corsetry, consisting of bras, briefs, bodies, suspender belts, bustiers or bodices, and basques. Underwear is an entirely different product from Beachwear as it is not purchased to be shown in public, but to make women more attractive and seductive in their intimate and private life.

The basic elements of a bra are: adjustable straps, underwire to help support the bust, padding (not always present) for a fuller and more compact bust, and a whole range of elastics of different thicknesses for greater comfort.

There are many kinds of briefs available on the market: Brazilian, thongs, tanga, culottes and high-waisted panties are all elasticated. The height of the waist can vary, depending on the uses for which the briefs are intended, but they are always thin and lightweight around the leg to facilitate movement.

In all the various forms of Lingerie, lace is the most widely used fabric. Among the most classic, refined and lightweight laces are Valenciennes and Chantilly, mostly produced in the historical factories of Calais in France, macramé and tombolo (also called "bobbin lace"), while the most popular is Sangallo lace, which is usually made of cotton using a shuttle weave. Cheaper, but still of excellent quality, are Rachel and Jacquardtronic lace that are the perfect substitute for the more expensive ones. Today, new technologies allow the production of an infinite range of soft, durable and super stretch lace.

Another essential base for making lingerie is tulle, ideal for creating transparencies, especially in corsetry. Like lace it was once used only in rigid form, but for more than half a century it has been an elasticated product with different weights and sizes and various levels of transparency depending on the requirements of the garment for which it will be used. Heavy tulles can also provide support, so they are widely used in models that have this function. Moreover, thanks to its high elasticity, it is often used as a base for intricate embroideries.

At the same time, embroidery on rigid tulle limits wearability and is therefore more suited to looser garments such as nightgowns or slips.

If you love extreme transparencies an innovative base for embroidery is tattoo effect tulle, a misleading name since it is actually a lightweight jacquard knit super sheer nylon stocking which, if embroidered on a nude-coloured background, gives this surprising effect.

Other essential materials include microfibres, special fabrics affording a high degree of elasticity and comfort, made both in shuttle weave and jersey knit, that can be perforated, embroidered and bonded with other materials using laser techniques to obtain extraordinary levels of transparency.

In addition, there is shiny stretch satin, not silk or polyester, as well as sheer voile (slightly more opaque than tulle) and sensitive fabric in its lighter versions, produced specifically for corsetry.

The range of materials on offer is vast: in recent years, technology has made great strides in this clothing sector too, while never neglecting its aesthetic sense which, together with wearability, is an essential added value for lingerie.

This book aims to inspire the creative imagination of underwear designers, offering models, patterns, colours and materials to create brand new and original collections.

Basic

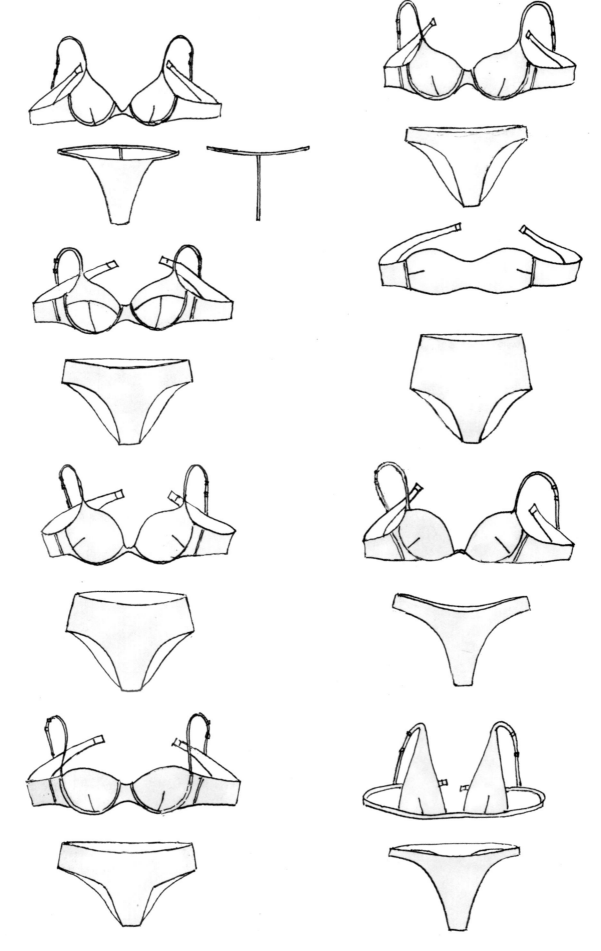

Plain basic body

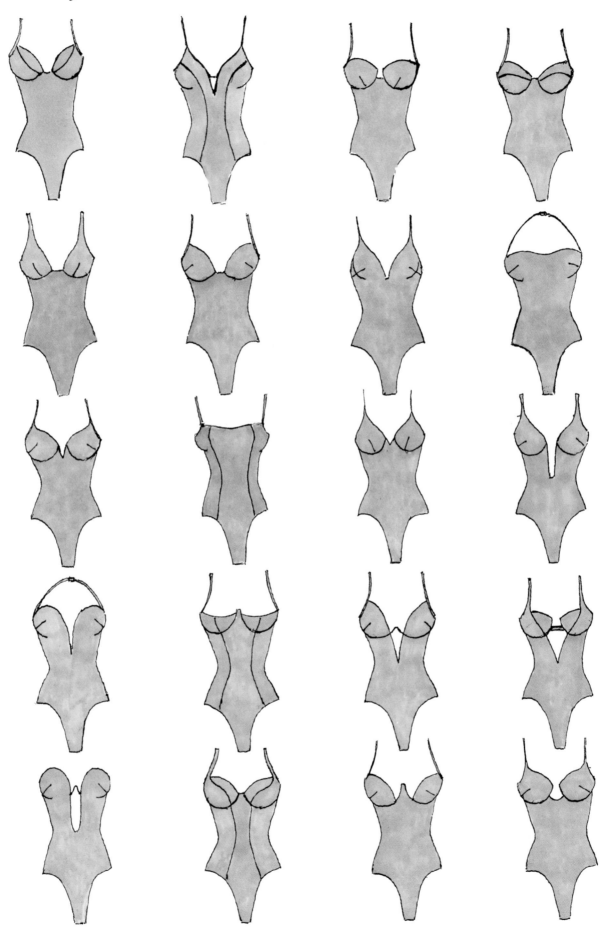

Lace bras

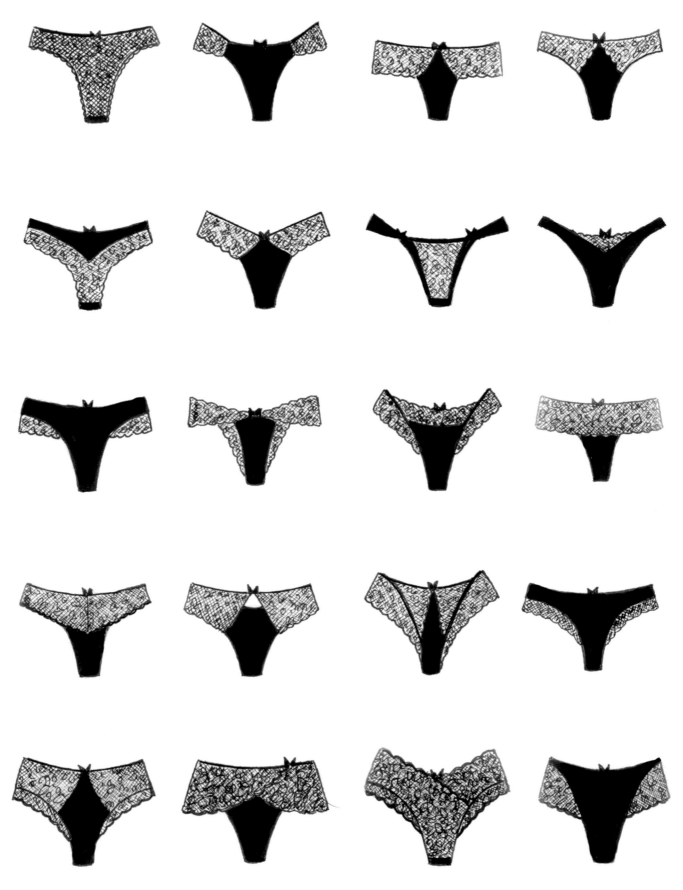

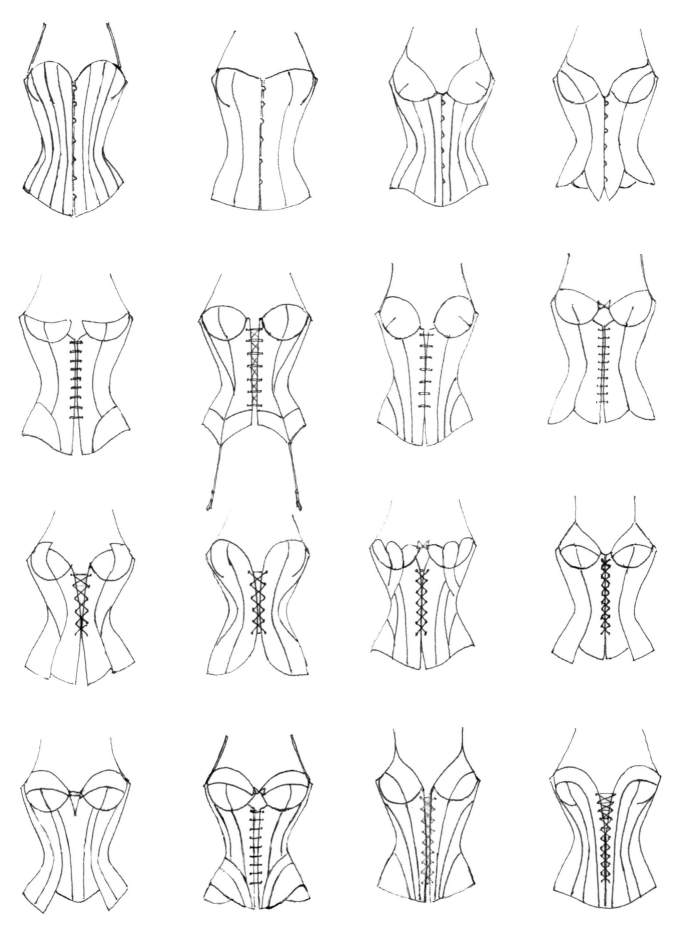

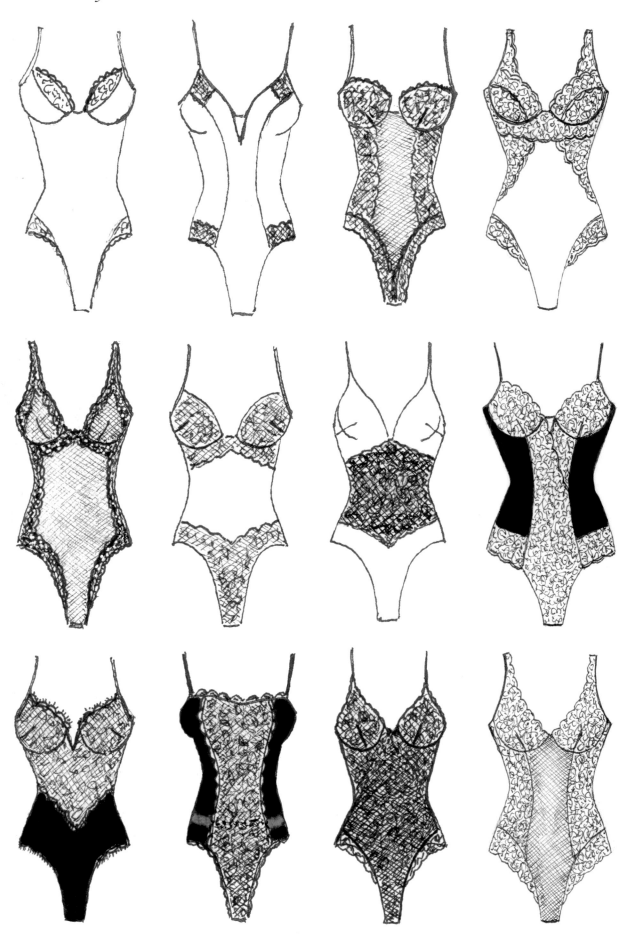

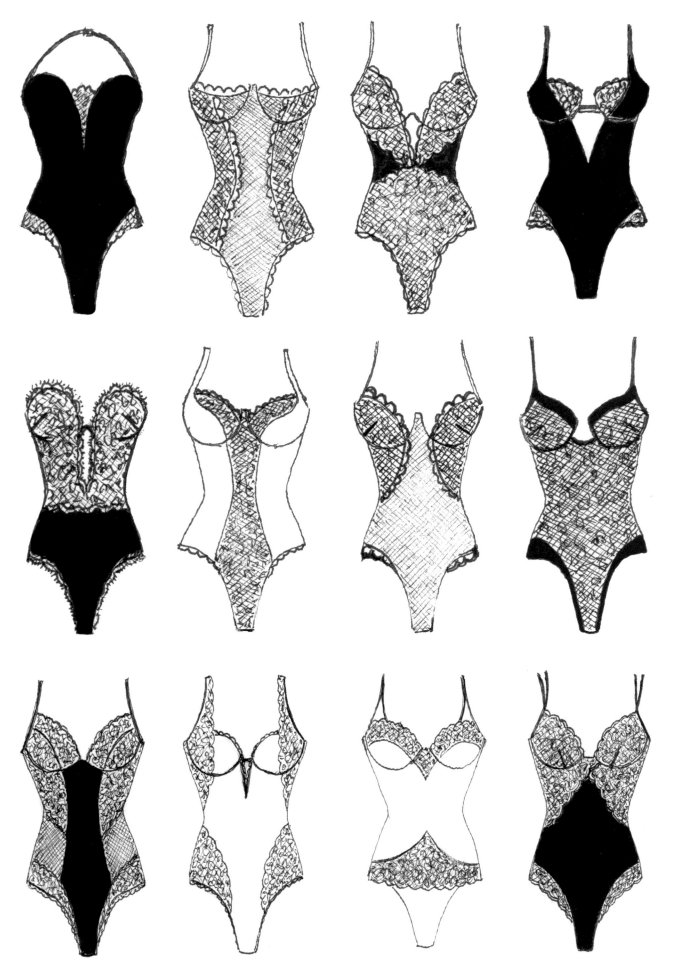

Basic long dressing gowns

Basic short dressing gowns

Basic slips

Basic long nightgowns

Basic underwear sets

Push up bra and
"Seagull Wing"
briefs.

Underwired
balcony bra and
medium-cut briefs.

Balcony bra with
underbust support
and "Brazilian"
briefs.

Underwired triangle
bra with or without
padding, and thong
briefs.

Non-wired triangle
bra without cups,
and culottes.

Push up bra and
thong briefs.

Underwired
bandeau balcony
bra with padding
and high-cut briefs.

Wired or non-wired
triangle bra without
padding, and culottes.

Underwired
elongated triangle
bra and low-cut
briefs.

Classic low-cut briefs and bra.

Classic medium-cut briefs and bra.

Low-waist culottes and bra.

Tanga and bra.

Classic bra and thong.

Brazilian briefs and bra.

Low-waist high-cut culottes and bra.

Bra and g-string.

Very high leg medium-cut briefs and bra.

Very high leg low-cut briefs in stretch voile with embroidery and bra.

Stretch voile lace bustier and high-cut briefs embroidered with microfibre.

Microfibre stretch lace for bra and medium-cut briefs.

Classic stretch silk satin basque with suspender belt and central hook fastening.

Strapless stretch lace and tulle basque without suspenders (briefs separate).

Basque with detachable suspenders. Central fastening with hidden hooks. Micro briefs separate.

27

Unstructured stretch microfibre
bandeau body.
Detachable suspenders.

Underwired body with stretch
microfibre push up cups.

Bra technical details

Underwired minimal elongated triangle bra without double effect cups. Dual stretch microfibre and tulle in the center and underbust.

Non-wired triangle bra without internal cups. Stretch tulle with polka dot embroidery.

Underwired bra with preformed cups (without darts).

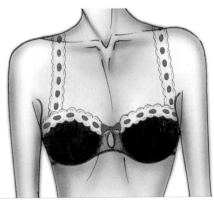

Single underwire balcony bra with inner lining.

Semi-padded (only under the half-bust cut) underwired balcony bra.

Padded balcony bra (internal cups and underwire).

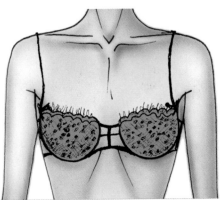

Padded bandeau bra with detachable shoulder straps and preformed cups (without darts and underwire).

Push up bra with macramé embroidery, padded with special nude-coloured cups that lift the bust considerably.

Padded balcony bra with lace decoration.

Stretch lace sets

Stretch lace and tulle body

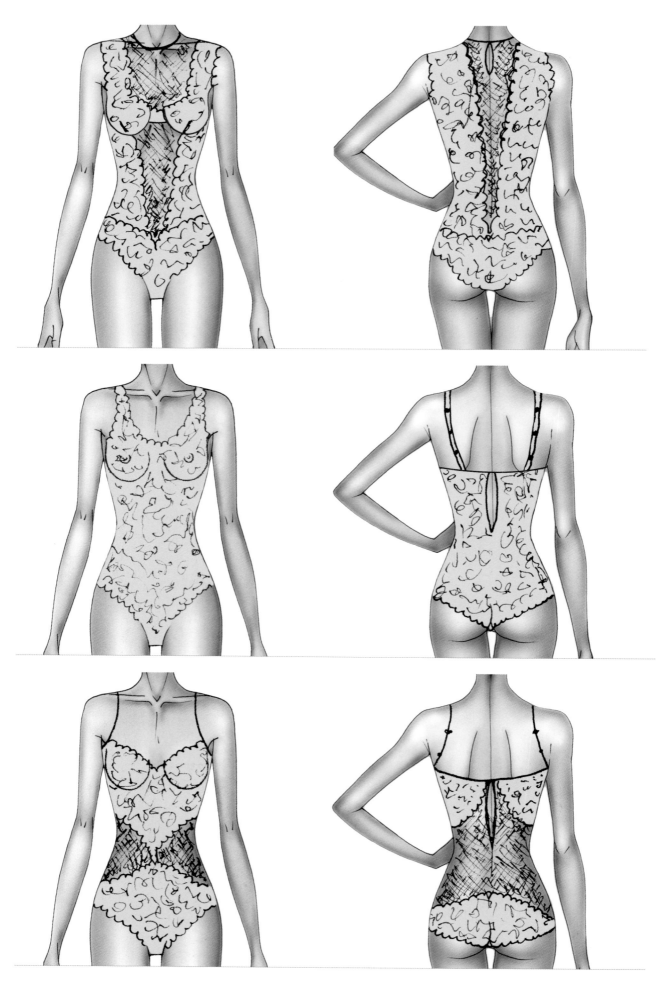

Stretch tulle bustier front and back.

Stretch tulle bra, briefs and suspender belt front and back.

Stretch tulle body front and back.

Bras, briefs and bodies

Stretch lace and tulle push up bra and briefs.

Underwired balcony bra, padded with stretch microfibre and stretch lace flounces. Low-cut briefs.

Stretch micro jacquard with chevrons and lace flounces for triangle bra and medium-cut briefs.

Stretch jacquard knit for bandeau bra and micro briefs. Brandy-coloured lining.

Underwired balcony bra with St. Gallen effect embroidery on microfibre. Valenciennes braiding.

Stretch microfibre and embroidered stretch tulle underwired balcony bra. Detachable shoulder straps and medium-cut briefs.

Triangle, culottes and suspender belt in printed stretch microfibre and stretch lace.

Unstructured elongated triangle bra and culottes in printed microfibre and stretch lace flounces.

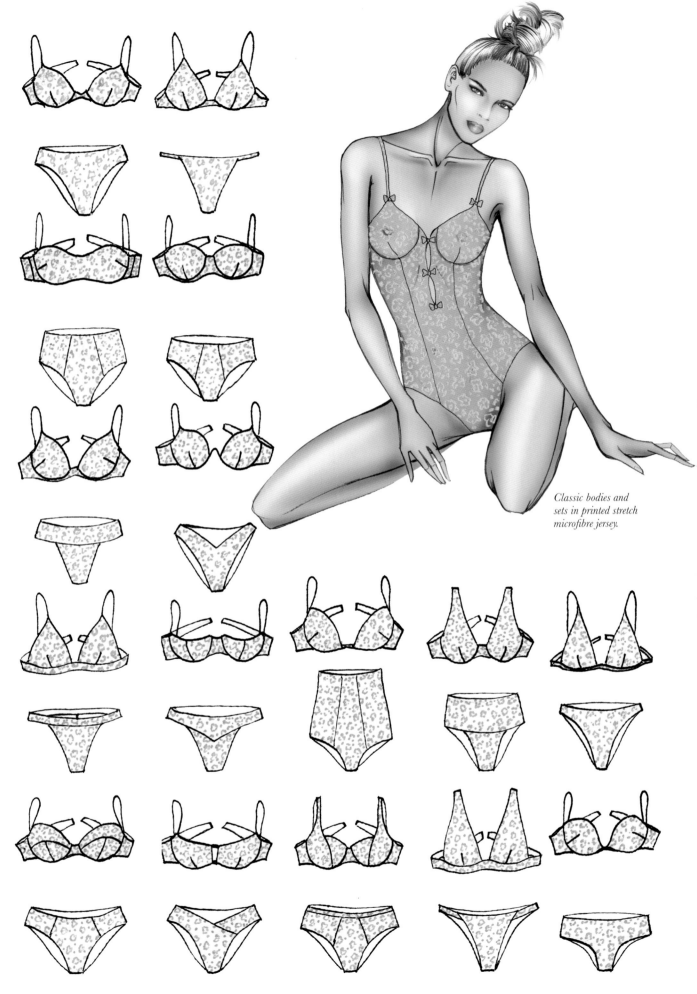

Classic bodies and sets in printed stretch microfibre jersey.

Dressing gowns, pyjamas, nightgowns

*Classic long interlock jacquard
dressing gown with Scottish
wool blend.
Internal placket, turned-up cuffs,
belt and pocket flaps in animal
print satin.*

*Short winter dressing gown with zip fastening
and side pockets. Quilted printed satin with
internal padding, acrylic jersey lining and
satin edging. Jacquard satin carré trim.*

Classic plain velvet dressing gown
with carré on the back. Pockets and
cuffs in multicoloured crochet knit.

Short printed fleece dressing gown with
satin quilted carré for the pockets, the
ruffles and the neck bow.

*Long printed velveteen shawl dressing
gown with satin bias trim.*

*Drop stitch jacquard knit viscose/wool blouse
with 1/1 rib stitch. Viscose/wool jersey
trousers with slit at the bottom.*

Modal cotton jersey pyjamas. Lace
inserts with beige and white braiding,
black satin ribbons and satin covered
buttons.

Chenille sleepsuit. Rib stitch collar
and cuffs with elastane. Zip and
flower inserts in embroidered tulle
(plastron n° 5).

43

Reverse print brushed fleece shawl pyjamas with 2/2 double rib stitch ruffles and decorated with satin ribbon. Plain brushed fleece trousers and collar.

Printed fleece pyjamas with large ring collar and 1/1 rib stitch cuffs with elastane.

Summer pyjamas in printed cotton muslin with St. Gallen embroidery ruffles with braiding

Short printed cotton jersey summer nightgown with ruffles and St. Gallen embroidery waistband braiding on cotton muslin.

45

Printed cotton creponne longuette nightgown with different kinds of embroidery, such as à jour and St. Gallen.

Short printed cotton interlock summer robe with lace drawstring waist and side pockets.

Short printed cotton jersey summer nightgown with lace flounces.

Plain cotton muslin longuette summer nightgown with lace and drawstring waist.

*Plain viscose/cotton
interlock long summer
nightgown with lace and
side pockets.*

*Printed cotton jersey summer
pyjamas with lace carré and
embroidery. Gold stars and silver
moon decoration plus printed
cotton canvas cats.*

Nightgown with snap button fastening. Embroidery and satin laser-cut motifs on wool blend interlock knit sleeves. Cloth body (shuttle). Trim and placket in the same material as the embroidery.

Printed cotton jersey summer pyjamas with 1/1 cotton and elastane rib stitch.

Printed cotton jersey summer pyjamas with embroidery and ladybird decoration. Contrasting polka dot motif.

The 1800s

Stretch lace and cage
effect set.

Underwired stretch lace balcony bra
with stretch cage-effect like the culottes,
suspender belt and gloves.

Stretch cage-effect lace basque.
Stretch tulle gloves with satin
ribbons.

Basque with lace suspender belt and underwired stretch cage-effect at the bust.

Long-sleeved carré non-wired body with stretch straps and lace.

Underwired sleeveless stretch lace body with stretch cage effect.

Front and back of a stretch lace and stretch satin body with lace-up closure, stretch straps and suspenders.

Front and back of a stretch lace and stretch satin bustier with stretch straps, culottes and suspenders.

51

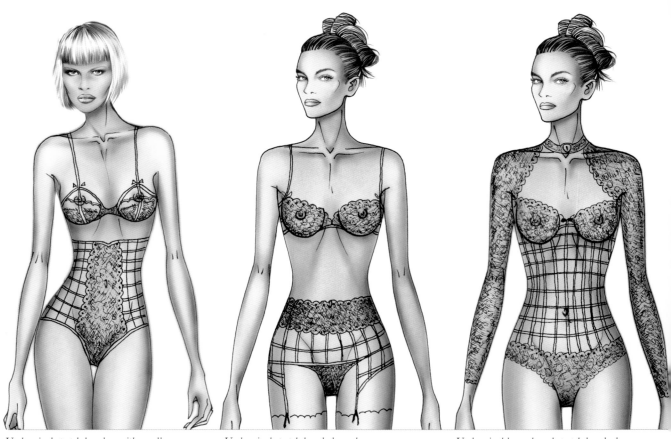

Underwired stretch lace bra with small
padding. Stretch lace fashion culottes with
stretch straps.

Underwired stretch lace balcony bra.
Suspender belt with built-in thong and stretch
cage-effect straps.

Underwired long-sleeved stretch lace body
with stretch cage effect.

Underwired stretch lace bra with stretch
straps. Suspender belt with built-in cage-
effect briefs.

Stretch lace bustier. Culottes with
cage-effect stretch straps.

Stretch lace plain voile nightgown
with satin ribbons.

▲ *Stretch lace and tulle long nightgown with satin in the bodice.*

◀ *Satin and embroidered tulle lounguette nightgown plus lace and flounces.*

▶ *Long velvet dressing gown with lace and satin ribbons.*

*Printed silk chiffon
nightsuit.*

*Chantilly lace and
stretch satin mini robe.*

*Short lace nightgown with stretch
straps and silk chiffon.*

Dark Lady

Underwired mesh and stretch strap bustier with embroidered motif.

Body with crossed and straight stretch straps. Underwired.

Body with crossed laser-cut straps.

Stretch lace and satin basque with suspenders, front fastening, underwired.

Long sleeve bustier with visible microfibre underwire and stretch mesh with high-cut culottes.

Retro basque with faux leather suspenders with contrasting stitching and mesh.

Stretch lace and tulle basque with detachable shoulder straps and suspenders flowers.

Underwired stretch microfibre and mesh sets.

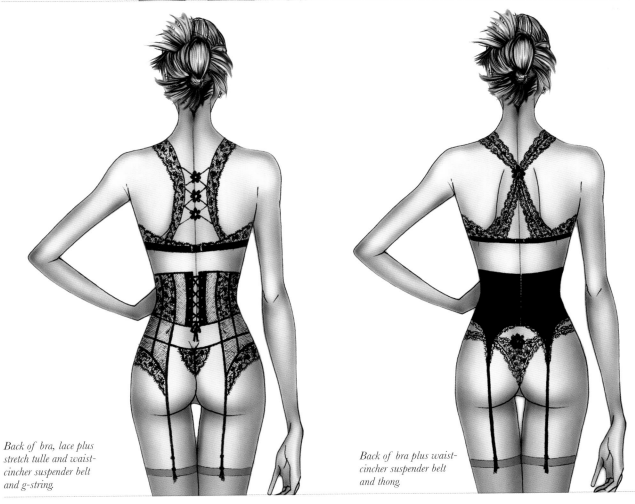

Back of bra, lace plus stretch tulle and waist-cincher suspender belt and g-string

Back of bra plus waist-cincher suspender belt and thong

Lace and tulle vest and
briefs with small macramé
flower and rhinestones.

Bustier and culotte. Embroidery on
nude tulle, black stretch mesh and
black tulle only on the culottes. Black
macramé flowers.

Long sleeve bustier with
microfibre underwire and
stretch mesh. Culottes with
suspenders made of the same
materials.

Laser-cut stretch faux
leather bustier.

Stretch faux leather basque, shaped in
metallic bronze, smaller silver lurex
thread macramé motif on the
shoulder strap and lace effect
lurex embroidery.

Stretch macramé body
with stretch microfibre
inserts, stretch
straps and macramé
geometric pattern.
Internal underwire.

Underwired stretch macramé
balcony bra. Stretch
microfibre on the centre bust
and on the briefs.

Underwired stretch macramè bra with stretch straps. Stretch microfibre side panels like the briefs.

Underwired stretch tulle and microfibre padded bra. Stretch straps like the suspender belt. Separate thong briefs.

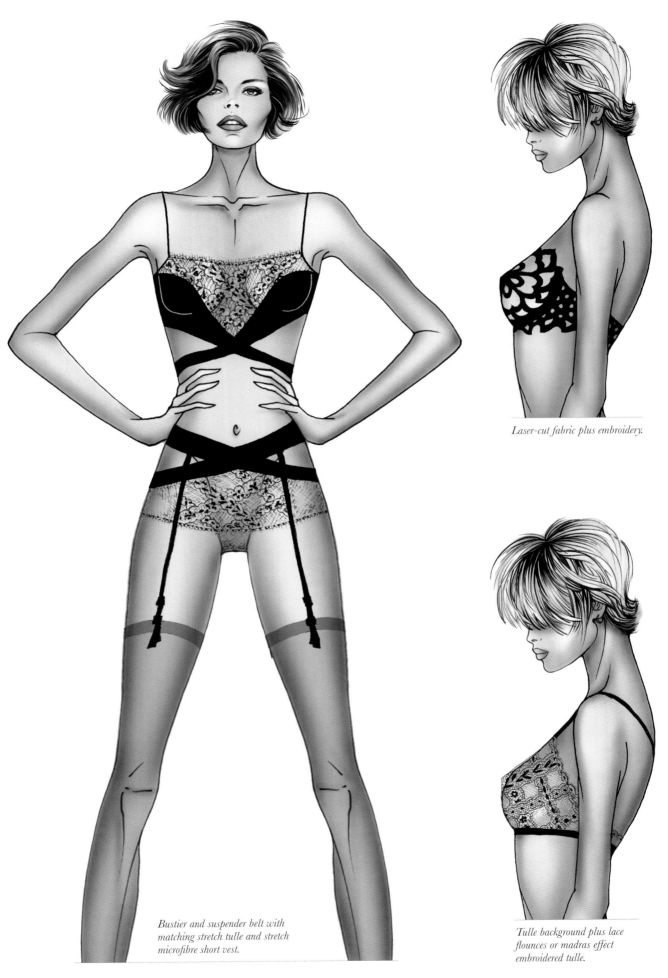

Laser-cut fabric plus embroidery.

Bustier and suspender belt with matching stretch tulle and stretch microfibre short vest.

Tulle background plus lace flounces or madras effect embroidered tulle.

*Macramé embroidery bandeau
bra on mesh or tulle background
decorated with micro rhinestones.
Detachable shoulder straps.*

*Embroidered silk voile fabric short
nightgown with embroidered flounces
and madras effect lace.*

*Embroidery on nude tulle plus black
stretch mesh and black stretch tulle.
Black macramé flowers.*

Underwired fashion padded bra with cups, plus waist-cincher with beaver-coloured stretch tulle suspenders and g-string, embroidered in black, plus black stretch tulle and mesh.

Stretch tulle and faux leather body with cornely effect embroidery.

Macramé embroidered body with small rhinestone decoration on mesh or tulle background.

Lounguette nightgown with silk satin front and stretch tulle back. Embroidery insert on nude tattoo background with strap effect on the side.

Dévoré voile long dressing gown with Chantilly lace and stretch satin waist band. Satin ribbons.

Stretch faux leather and lace set.
Small studs on bust and briefs.

Fashion body in stretch faux
leather and stretch lace at
the waist. Small studs and
suspenders.

Heavy control satin or stretch faux leather bustier and high waist culottes (shapewear).

Stretch satin mini slip with laser-cut and stretch voile.

Push up bra with briefs and suspender belt.

Stretch faux leather padded bra
with matching briefs.

Ultra-lightweight stretch faux
leather basque with lace and
stretch tulle.

Stretch faux leather body with
detachable suspenders.

Stretch satin mini slip with lace
and stretch tulle inserts.

Underwired stretch faux leather
bra with straight cups and
fashion culottes.

Lace body with visible elastic straps.

Basque body with detachable suspenders. All in stretch lace and faux leather.

*Stretch voile and
lace underskirt.*

*Stretch tulle and stretch
satin mini underskirt with
embroidered flounces.*

▲ *Stretch faux leather and pleated tulle
basque with suspenders, with detachable
shoulder straps and collar (separate briefs).*

◄ *Nude stretch voile basque with
suspenders and small macramés. Front
hook fastening.*

71

Bustier and culottes
with stretch faux leather
straps. Stretch tulle in
the culottes.

Short shawl robe with
macramé embroidery
on mesh background.
Satin sash.

Animal print dévoré effect voile mini nightgown with satin embroidery and ribbons.

Animal print dévoré effect stretch voile bandeau bra, waist-cincher suspender belt and briefs.

Dévoré effect voile sleepsuit, animal print with stretch lace trim.

Super crop long-sleeve shoulder plus top and stretch lace high waist leggings with nude stretch tulle straps.

High technology

Laser-cut bra and briefs plus
embroidery.

Stretch microfibre and stretch
voile mini slip.

Basque, embroidery on lace
plus laser-cut, stretch microfibre
background fabric, jacquard damask.

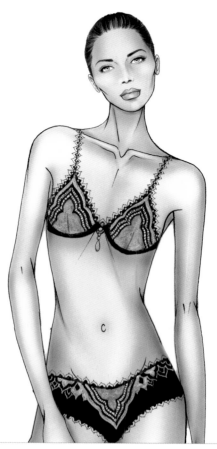

Laser-cut printed satin on stretch lace basque.

Underwired embroidered triangle bra with gold lurex fabric decoration, like on the culottes.

Front and back laser-cut body with lurex embroidery.

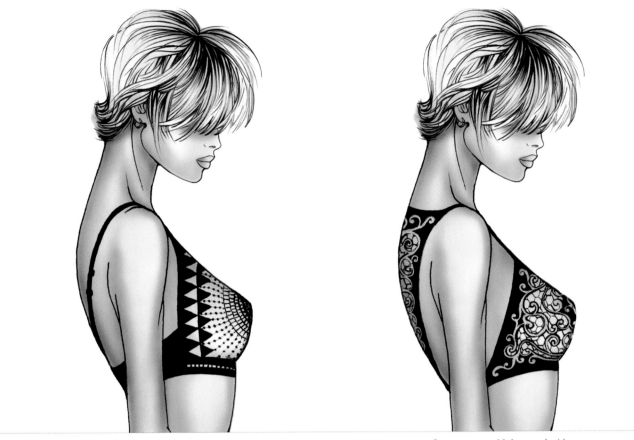

Macramé embroidery.

Laser-cut top with lurex embroidery.

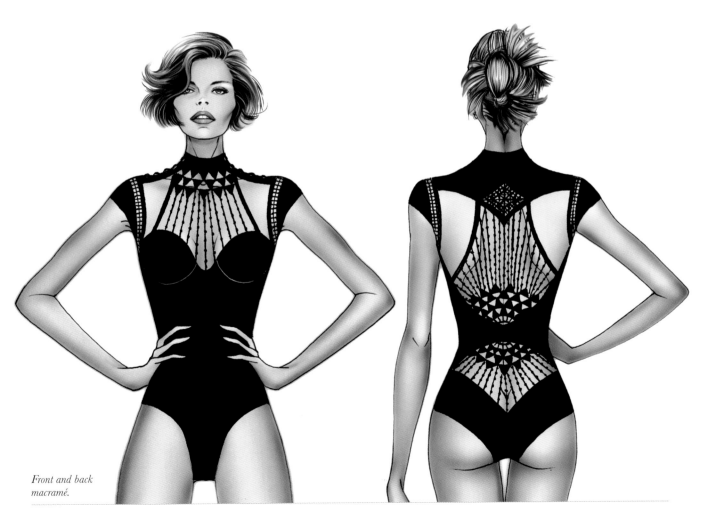

Front and back macramé.

Macramé embroidery top and briefs with suspenders.

Macramé embroidery body.

Laser-cut piping insert plus lace.

*Laser-cut set with
lurex embroidery.*

*Laser-cut faux leather and lace push
up bra, waist cincher with suspenders
and briefs*

Laser-cut body with
metallic foil decoration.

Embroidery with
laser-cut decoration.

Slip with laser-cut decoration on stretch voile plus stretch satin or other material.

Laser-cut ultra-lightweight stretch faux leather and graduated silver foil body.

*Parisian slip. Embroidery with
laser-cut decoration.*

*Embroidery with laser-cut decoration.
Bustier and Brazilian high-cut briefs*

*Underwired
perforated macramé
embroidery and
stretch tulle bra
with laser-cut
butterfly motif.
Matching briefs.*

*Macramé embroidered
body with small laser-cut
decoration.*

Macramé embroidered
microfibre bustier and
briefs with laser-cut
decoration.

Body with black and silver
animalier embroidery on a nude
stretch tulle background. Black
stretch microfibre with silver
zebra stripe embroidery.

▾ Macramé embroidered
top and culottes with
small laser-cut decoration.
Embroidered stretch tulle
only for the culottes.

Lace effect antique gold foil print stretch
microfibre body with cashmere motifs.

Stripes and polka dot dévoré voile short summer pyjamas. Red laser-cut tulle floral embroidery on a super sheer tattoo background.

Dévoré voile mini nightgown plus stretch lace.

Short wool cloth winter dressing gown with laser-cut faux leather trim and wool fringes. Corded wool belt with tassels and side pockets.

Velvet effect floral dévoré jacquard pyjamas with stretch lace polka dot flounces.

Short winter dressing gown in two fabrics: printed jersey inside and plain jersey outside. Lightweight padding between the two fabrics. Side pockets and contrasting satin edging.

Laser-cut satin short summer dressing gown with embroidered St. Gallen motifs.

Tattoo effect

Lurex lace triangle bra with decorative motif.

Underwired embroidered bra.

Body with embroidered motif side insert.

Embroidered internal underwire padded top.

All over embroidery body.

Body with embroidered motif on the sleeves and back.

Outerwear body with
cornelly embroidery on a
tattoo background plus lace
and microfibre.

Bustier and briefs with
cornelly embroidery insert
on a tattoo background plus
striped tulle.

Body with cornelly embroidery
inserts on a tattoo background
and striped tulle.

Microfibre vest with
embroidery on a tattoo
background and stretch tulle.

Front and back of a body with embroidery on a tattoo background (super sheer nude knit) plus small stretch tulle insert.

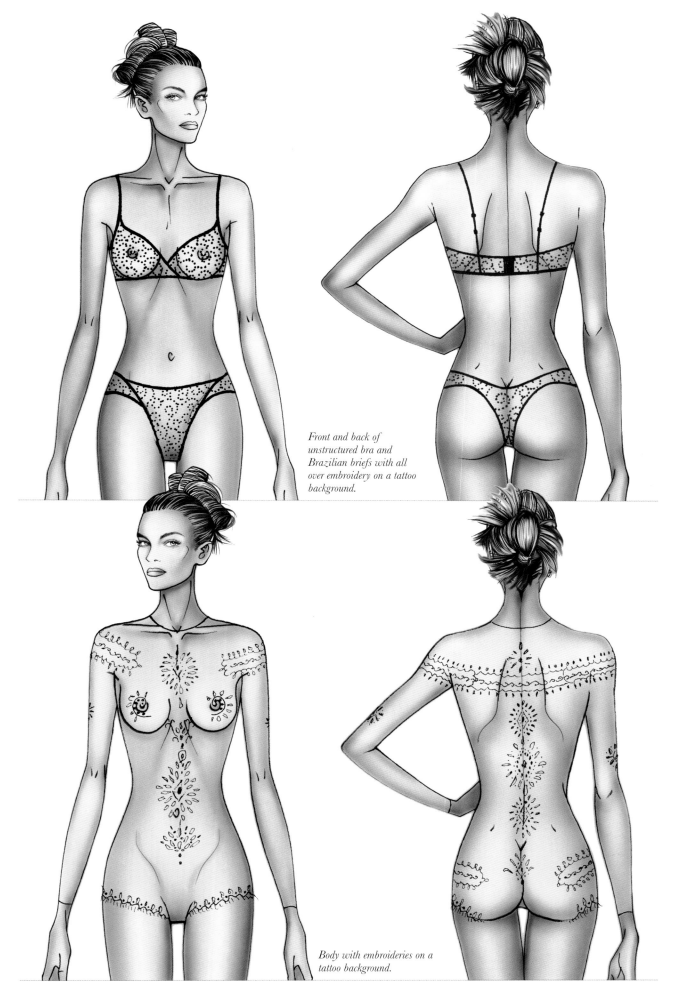

Front and back of unstructured bra and Brazilian briefs with all over embroidery on a tattoo background.

Body with embroideries on a tattoo background.

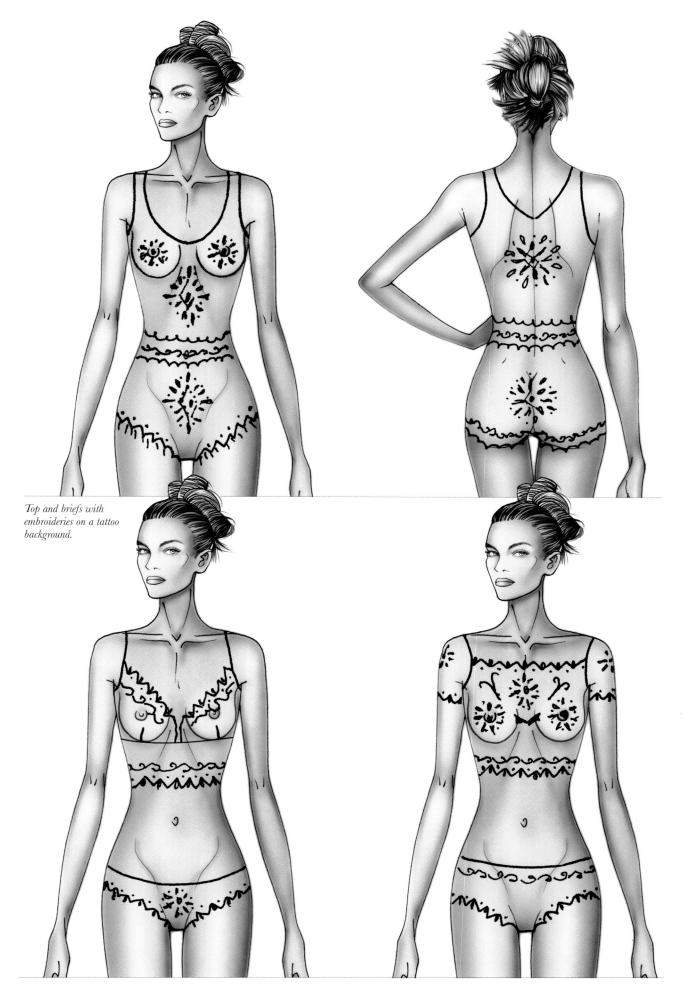

Top and briefs with
embroideries on a tattoo
background.

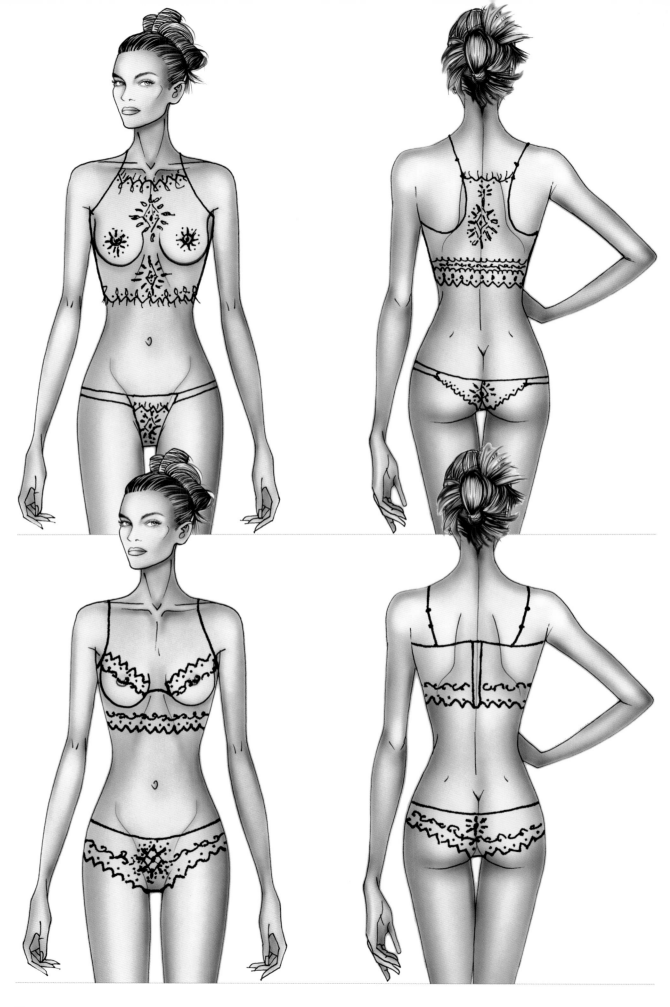

Stretch lace lounguette nightgown plus tulle on a nude background with black macramé effect embroidery.

Nude tulle sleepsuit with black embroidery and black stretch lace.

Underwired bra with embroidery on a tattoo background and high-cut briefs.

Underwired padded bra. Embroidery on a tattoo background and medium-cut briefs.

Underwired bra and culottes with embroidery on a tattoo background.

Silk lingerie

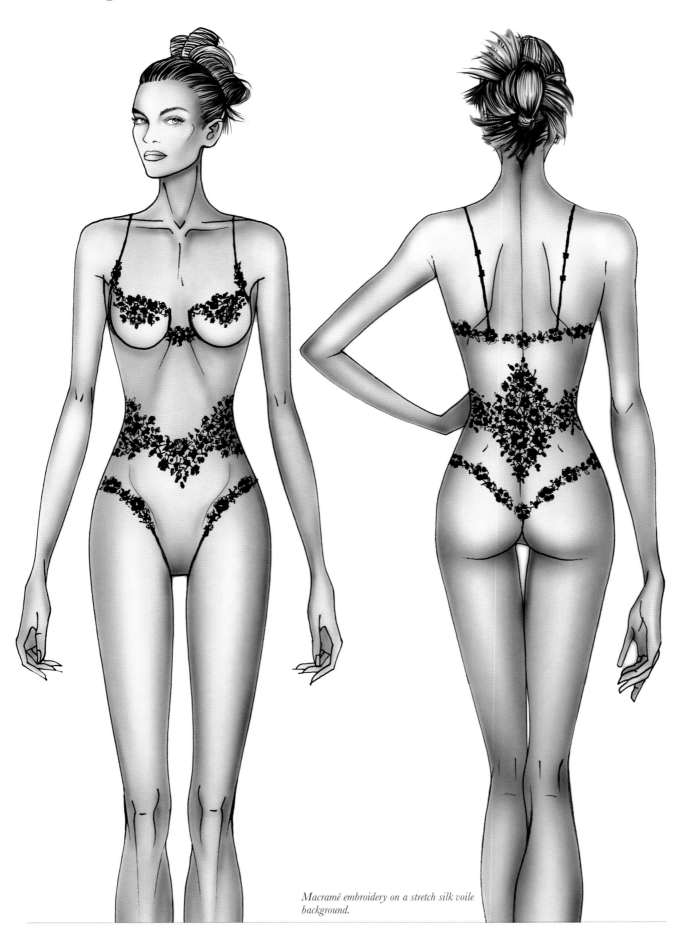

Macramé embroidery on a stretch silk voile background.

*Stretch silk voile and stretch tulle sets with
macramé embroideries.*

Stretch silk fashion bra with straps in the same fabric and embroidered tulle on the bust and briefs.

Bustier plus stretch silk culottes with chantilly rigid lace inserts.

Stretch tulle bra with
macramé flounce and
matching briefs.

Stretch silk unstructured
triangle bra and briefs
with macramé plastron.

Stretch silk body
with underwired
bust and macramé
flounce motifs.

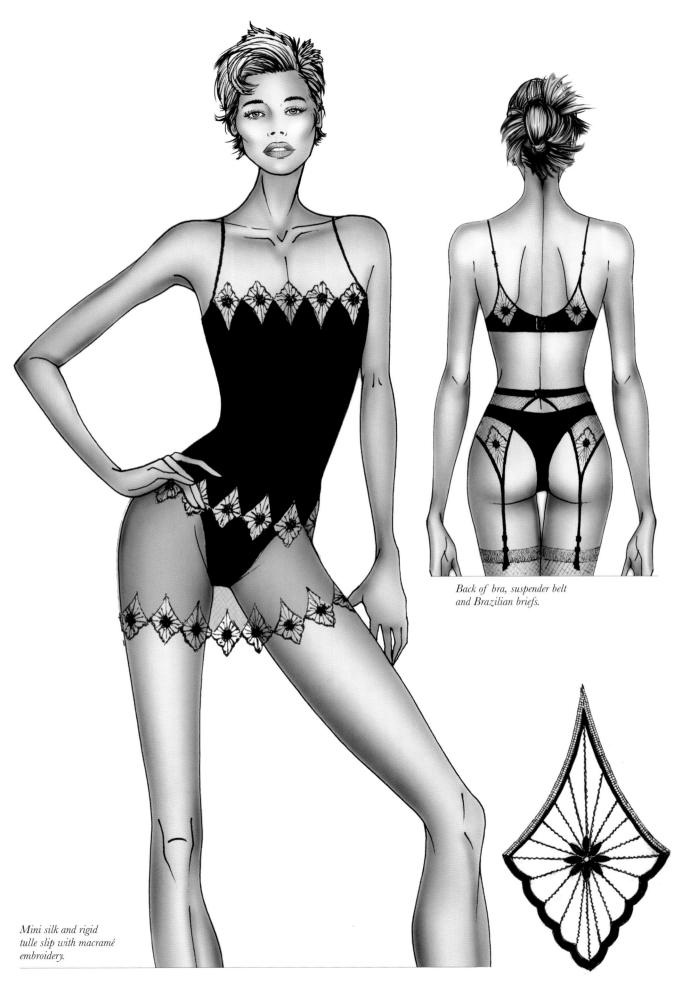

*Back of bra, suspender belt
and Brazilian briefs.*

*Mini silk and rigid
tulle slip with macramé
embroidery.*

Underwired stretch silk fashion body with padded bust, stretch lace and suspenders.

Underwired stretch
silk triangle bra with
chantilly rigid lace.
Thong briefs.

Stretch embroidered
tulle body with motifs
and stretch silk.

Stretch tulle body with
embroidered tulle flounce
and stretch silk for bust
and briefs. Small central
macramé motif.

Stretch microfibre fashion body
with stretch lace flounces.
Underwired bust and lining.

Silk satin basque with internal
ribs, macramé shawl collar
and detachable shoulder straps.
Brazilian briefs with detachable
suspenders.

*Internal underwired
bust stretch lace and
microfibre fashion bra
with matching briefs.*

*Small macramé
plastron decoration.*

*Stretch tulle and stretch
silk mini slip with different
types of lace.*

Stretch velvet basque with embroidered stretch tulle and macramé long sleeves. Macramé and embroidered stretch tulle high-cut culottes like the sleeves.

Basque with silk satin suspender belt, stretch lace and macramé motif at the centre of the waist. Briefs separate.

Macramé embroidered silk and tulle, and voile longuette nightgown.

*Stretch silk and
stretch lace underskirt.
Padded balcony bra.*

*Mini slip in two types of lace:
one more transparent and the
other more opaque.*

*Mini silk satin slip with lace
and stretch tulle, embroidered
on the bust.*

*Mini slip with lace, silk satin and
stretch lace flounces.*

*Mini slip with lace, à jour and
silk inserts.*

▲ *Lace mini slip with stretch lace and tulle flounce.*

◀ *Lace mini slip plus embroidery on voile and lace flounce.*

▶ *Black stretch tulle mini slip with black embroidery inserts on nude stretch tulle plus lace.*

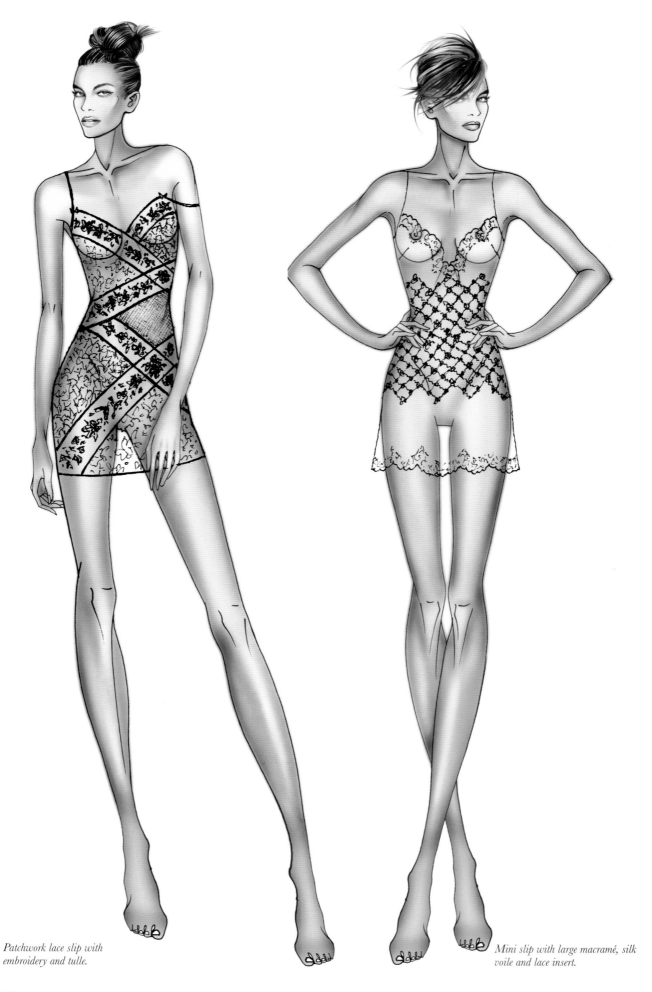

Patchwork lace slip with embroidery and tulle.

Mini slip with large macramé, silk voile and lace insert.

Long-sleeve body with
plumetis effect tulle plus
various laces or embroidery
and stretch silk inserts.

Stretch silk long
nightgown with different
types of embroidery on
stretch tulle.

*Basque with stretch
satin suspenders and
embroidery inserts.*

*Ultra-lightweight embroidered
silk voile short nightgown,
plus lace and embroidered
silk. Nude-coloured briefs.*

Underwired embroidered
stretch silk voile bra and
culottes plus lace and silk.

Short nightgown with
ultra-lightweight silk
lace fabric background
and silk lace flounces.

Ultra-lightweight silk lace
and stretch lace body with
ultra-lightweight silk lace
flounces.

Ultra-lightweight silk
lace background plus
silk lace flounce.

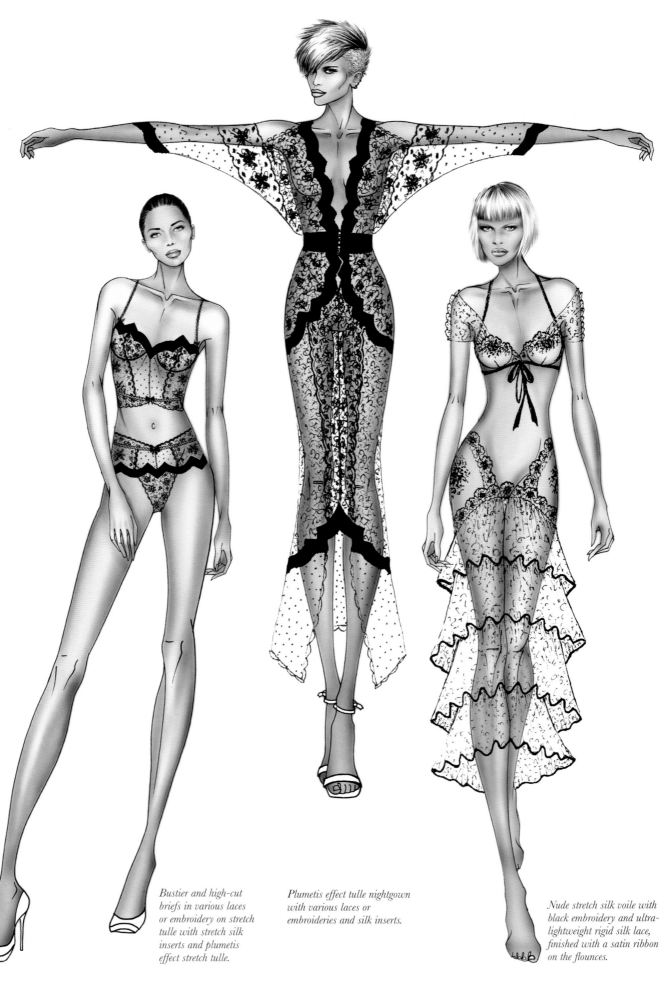

Bustier and high-cut
briefs in various laces
or embroidery on stretch
tulle with stretch silk
inserts and plumetis
effect stretch tulle.

Plumetis effect tulle nightgown
with various laces or
embroideries and silk inserts.

Nude stretch silk voile with
black embroidery and ultra-
lightweight rigid silk lace,
finished with a satin ribbon
on the flounces.

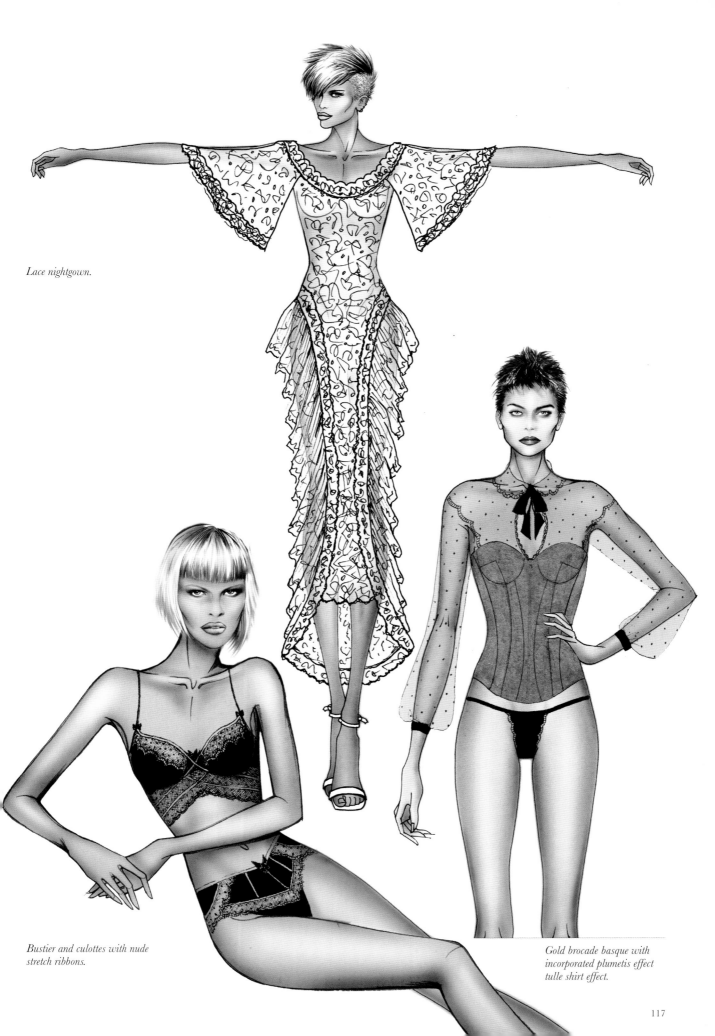

Lace nightgown.

*Bustier and culottes with nude
stretch ribbons.*

*Gold brocade basque with
incorporated plumetis effect
tulle shirt effect.*

117

Mini vest with polka dot embroidery on a nude plumetis effect tulle and stretch silk background.

Underwired polka dot stretch tulle bra and stretch silk (small strip on the side).

Stretch polka dot tulle and stretch silk push up bra.

Underwired triangle bra with suspenders (polka dot stretch tulle and lace).

Polka dot tulle and stretch lace Parisian mini slip.

Underwired padded balcony bra with internal cups. Lace and silk briefs with a motif on the front and lace on the back like on the side of the bra.

Nude stretch silk voile push up bra and low-cut culottes with black macramé effect embroidery.

Underwired stretch silk voile balcony bra with black macramé effect embroidery plus classic briefs.

Underwired nude stretch tulle balcony bra and briefs with plumetis effect small black polka dots.

121

Underwired embroidered stretch tulle plus smooth stretch tulle semi-padded balcony bra and briefs.

Stretch embroidered tulle and smooth stretch tulle for the underwired balcony bra and briefs.

Mini lace, pleated voile and tulle vest with satin ribbons.

Body - basque with detachable suspenders in lace or embroidery of various kinds and plumetis effect tulle.

Nightgown with embroidered flounce on stretch tulle plus silk lace and plumetis effect voile.

123

Mini Parisian slip in a mix
of lace and embroidery.

Plumetis effect nude tulle body
with detachable suspenders and
lace shoulders.

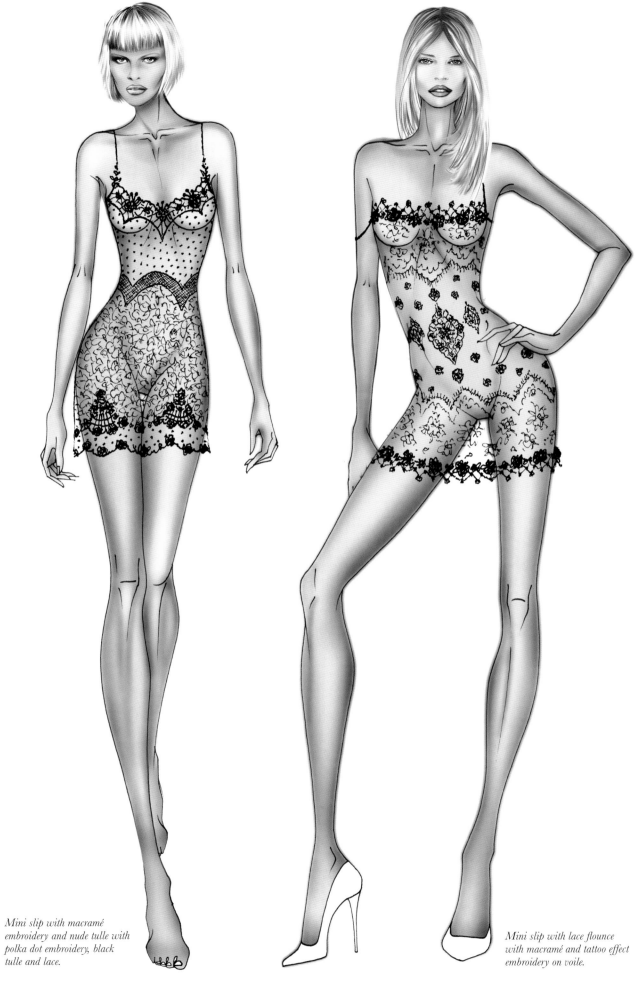

*Mini slip with macramé
embroidery and nude tulle with
polka dot embroidery, black
tulle and lace.*

*Mini slip with lace flounce
with macramé and tattoo effect
embroidery on voile.*

Printed silk satin kimono.

*Underwired padded body with
stretch silk cups and stretch polka
dot tulle. Nude stretch ribbons.*

Silk satin shawl open pyjamas. Mock neck,
lace sleeve and trouser inserts. Buttons with
rhinestones at the neck.

Short viscose velveteen dressing gown
with macramé lace sleeves. Silver jewel
snap buttons.

Bridal

*Macramé bustier with stretch tulle
and lace flounce.*

Mini silk satin slip in with macramé and lace embroidery.

Satin longuette nightgown with macramé rose embroidery. Tulle in the centre of the bodice, lace flounce and silk voile.

*Stretch lace bustier with
small macramé border.*

*Stretch tulle body embroidered
on the front with macramé on
the back, armhole and leghole.*

Voile babydoll with macramé.
Silk satin culottes.

Silk voile longuette nightgown
with macramé lace (or leavers).

Long silk voile dressing gown
with lace and macramé
embroidery.

Underskirt with embroidered
organza flounces and top.

Short stretch lace and silk
voile or chiffon nightgown.

Long voile and silk satin
dressing gown with small
macramé rose decoration.

Embroidery on stretch silk with small jewel accessories with rhinestones.

Stretch lace body.

Basque with macramé and voile embroidery.

Example of bicoloured macramé rose embroidery plastrons.

Underwired bra with cups, stretch silk satin and stretch voile waist-cincher suspender belt and briefs with macramé rose embroidery.

Stretch lace and silk satin underskirt.

Stretch silk satin and bicoloured stretch lace basque with detachable shoulder and suspenders. Separate lace briefs.

Embroidered stretch silk satin and stretch voile bustier and culottes.

Silk satin and bicoloured lace push up bra and culottes.

Silk and lace longuette nightgown.

Bicoloured lace longuette kimono dressing gown, silk trim and sash.

138

*Silk and à jour satin
basque and briefs.*

*Silk voile and lace short
open nightgown.*

Silk chiffon pyjamas with embroideries.

Silk satin pyjamas with mandarin collar and rigid chantilly lace. Jewel buttons.

Pleated voile shawl dressing gown
with lace trim. Satin sash. Fuchsia
and black lace large shawl collar
bodice with black satin lining

Crêpe de chine with rigid
and à jour lace inserts.

Silk voile triangle bra,
waist-cincher suspender belt
and briefs, silk satin and à
jour trim.

Body with embroidery on
stretch silk voile.

142

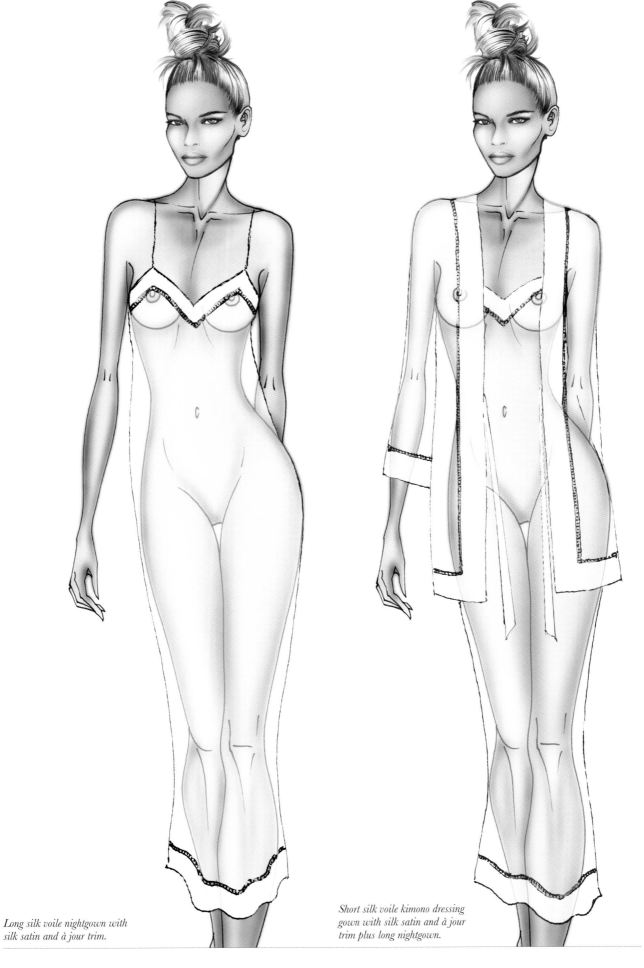

Long silk voile nightgown with silk satin and à jour trim.

Short silk voile kimono dressing gown with silk satin and à jour trim plus long nightgown.

St Valentine's Day

Lace body with two designs in stretch silk and tulle.

Stretch lace and silk bra, waist-cincher suspender belt and briefs.

Stretch satin body with suspenders with animal-print embroidered stretch tulle.

Stretch mesh bandeau bra with animalier embroidery plus macramé hearts with small rhinestones.

Stretch mesh bustier with animalier embroidery
and macramé hearts with small rhinestones.

Stretch microfibre body
with stretch lace flounce.

Basque with suspenders, stretch satin
and stretch mesh or tulle briefs.

Underwired padded balcony bra.
Stretch satin thong decorated
with macramé hearts and small
rhinestones.

Laser-cut heart design stretch satin with
nude lining, detachable shoulder straps
with micro rhinestones.

147

Stretch satin mini slip with
animalier embroidered
stretch tulle.

Stretch voile bustier with animalier
embroidered tulle insert and micro
briefs with silver lurex thread seams
and topstitching.

Unstructured stretch microfibre and macramé lace triangle bra. Shoulder straps with beads and metal rings. Centre bust and thong with ring fastener and clip-on pendant. Detachable red bead belt.

Beachwear

Beachwear encompasses a wide range of clothing such as sarongs, beach dresses, shorts, tops, and swimsuits, the real stars of beach fashion.

Already used by the Romans, this garment was usually an everyday item of clothing, but it was rarely worn since in ancient times bathing in the sea was still not a widespread activity and washing in the public baths was generally done unclothed.

From the mid-18th century, when the custom of going to the beach was growing in popularity, rather chaste bathing suits began to appear, composed of a vest top and long drawers. From then on, the swimsuit gradually evolved and models aimed at various water sports, such as swimming and rowing, were increasingly being developed, but mainly, more comfortable solutions for leisure time activities were being attempted.

In 1946, the French tailor Louis Reard created the first two-piece, renamed "Bikini" as in the Marshall Islands' atoll; these were garments made with non-elasticised shuttle fabrics, later replaced by jersey and elastomers, the most widely used of which was lycra, a yarn produced by Dupont. Its invention led to a real revolution in the field of beachwear thanks to its many properties, and its particular structure made it soft to the touch, breathable, shaping, and quick dryingo.

Unlike underwear, where black predominates, the colour of seduction par excellence, beachwear is characterised by a riot of colours, prints, quirky accessories and eye-catching embroideries.

Lycra is the basic material used to make swimwear. There are many different types of varying weight depending on the wearability needs of the garments. The heaviest (about 70 grams upwards) are intended for control swimsuits, while the lighter ones are used for all the other kinds. It is available both in a glossy version, with a silky appearance like satin, and in a matt version.

Of course other interesting materials are also used, the best known and most popular being microfibre which is produced in different weights. Opaque in appearance, it is very comfortable, stretchy, and soft, practically like a second skin. Equally important due to its remarkable characteristics and versatility is sensitive fabric, a unique high-tech product made in Italy.

Thanks to the most recent and innovative technologies, the resources for creating a beautiful swimsuit are now truly endless: laser-cut embroidery and metallic effect decoration, and plasma treatment are just a few, giving an excellent result from the technical and aesthetic point of view.

Digital printing has also brought about considerable improvements: the colours used are now limitless and the reproduction of an idea follows the photographic process, with results that are exceptionally faithful to the design. Times have also changed when it comes to the creation of original designs which are now rarely put on paper (and therefore handmade), and in most cases collections are created by computer and directly printed onto cuts of fabric. The digitisation of design has considerably reduced production times and, consequently, related costs.

Like in corsetry, some upper parts of swimsuits, both one and two-piece, are wired and often also have detachable or attached inner cups (light padding) for support and to make even smaller busts appear fuller. Alternatively, there are unstructured swimming costumes made without any kind of internal support, but simply lined with a lightweight stretch knit to stop the garment becoming embarrassingly see-through when wet, especially in lighter colours.

As for modelling, every kind of physical shape is catered for: the one-piece with different neckline and leg cuts, the bikini (or two-piece) in all its forms, the most classic of which are defined according to the model of the upper part and include the triangle, the bandeau, the push-up, and the balcony, with or without underwire or padding. Briefs are freely matched by the consumer and include thongs (the smallest), Brazilians (very high cut on the back), tangas, low, medium or high-cut briefs, and many others.

For several years now this item of clothing has undergone incredible transformations: the application of colourful rhinestones and other jewels, spangles and metallic studs, highly elaborate macramé embroidery inserts on backgrounds that can be plain or printed with iridescent and glittering plasma treatments, have turned it into a truly precious gem!

Matching the swimsuits and known as "beach apparel", there are various coordinated accessories such as sarongs, beach towels, bags and sandals, which complete the holiday collection.

Apart from the general ideas mentioned above, the content of this book is intended to be of help and inspiration to those interested in this particular field of fashion.

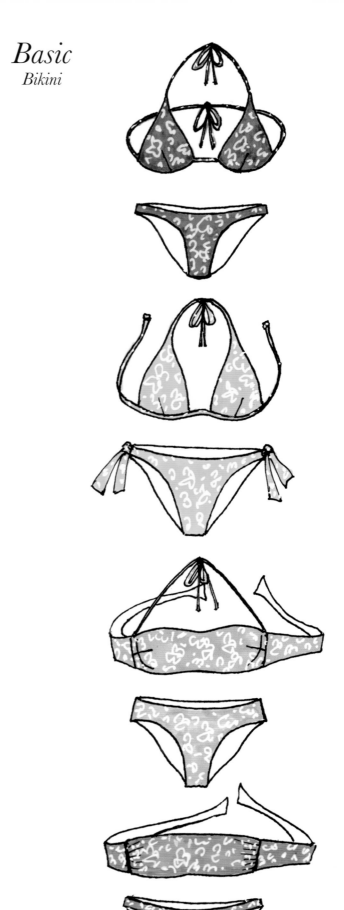

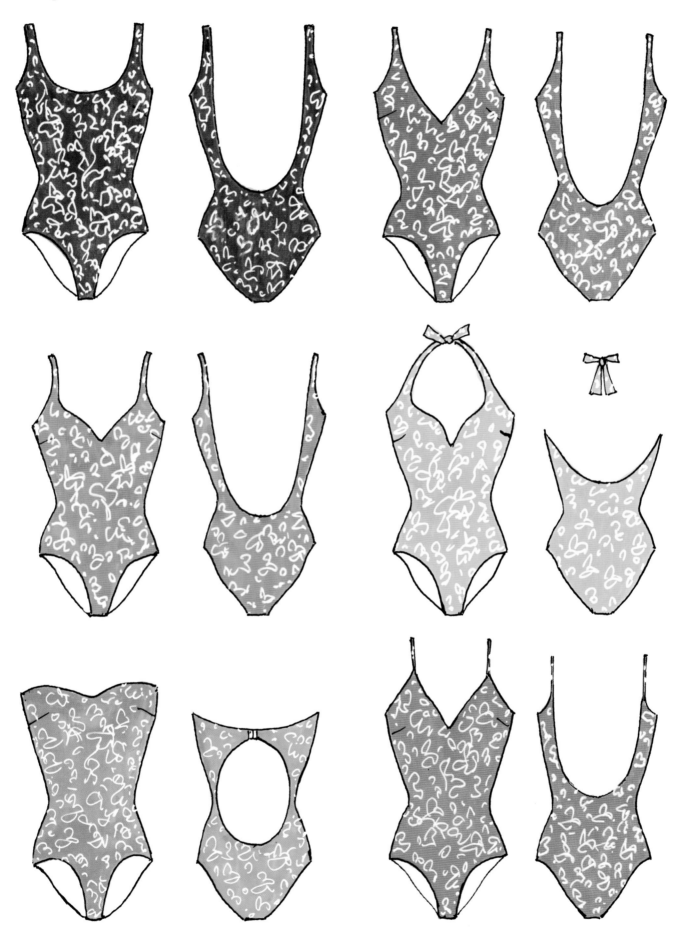

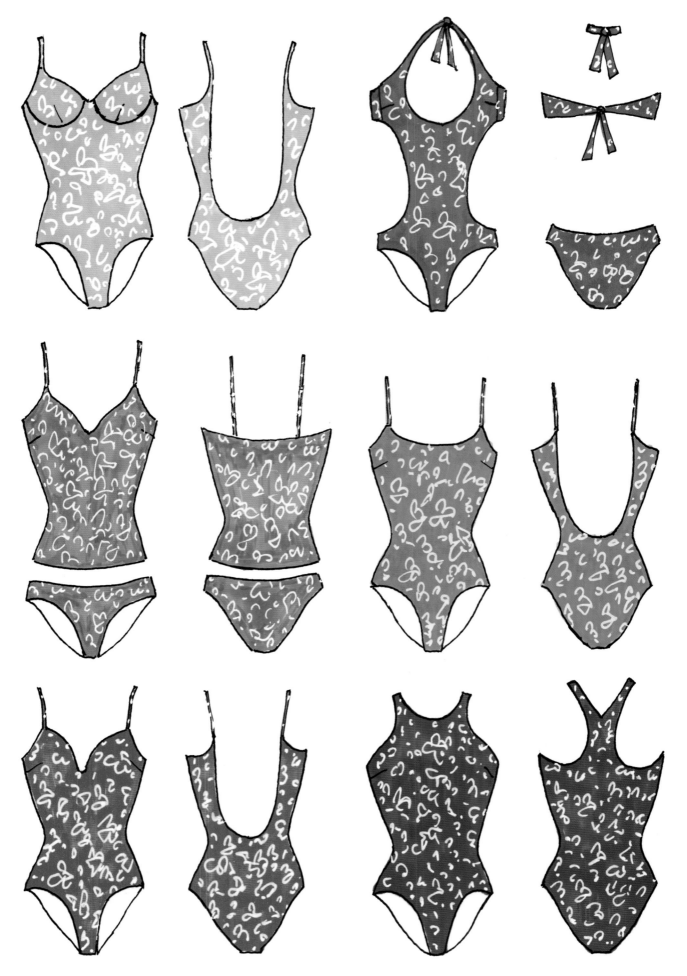

Pop Series

Basic black and white swimsuits with rings

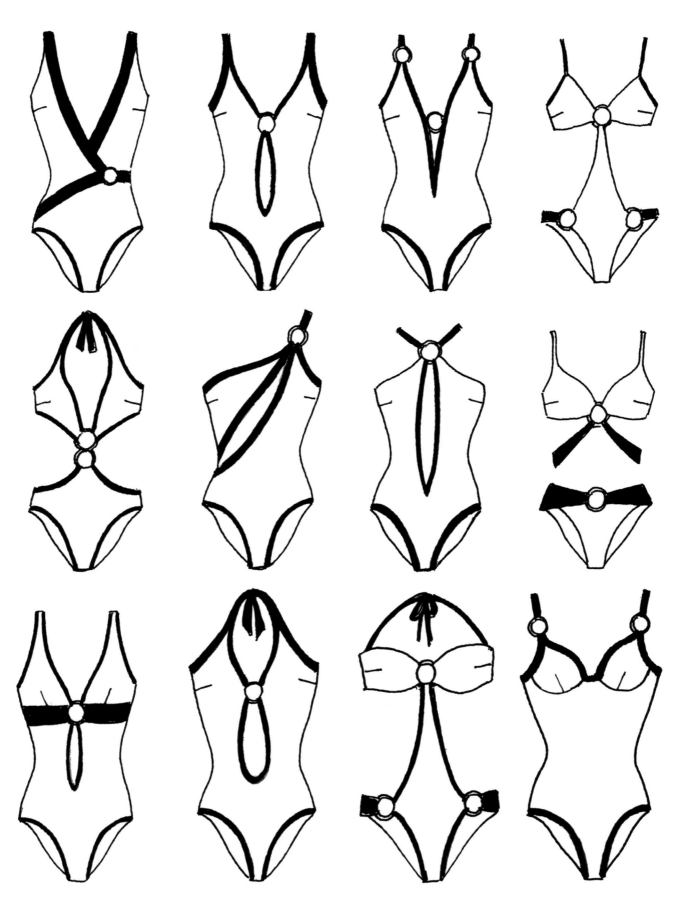

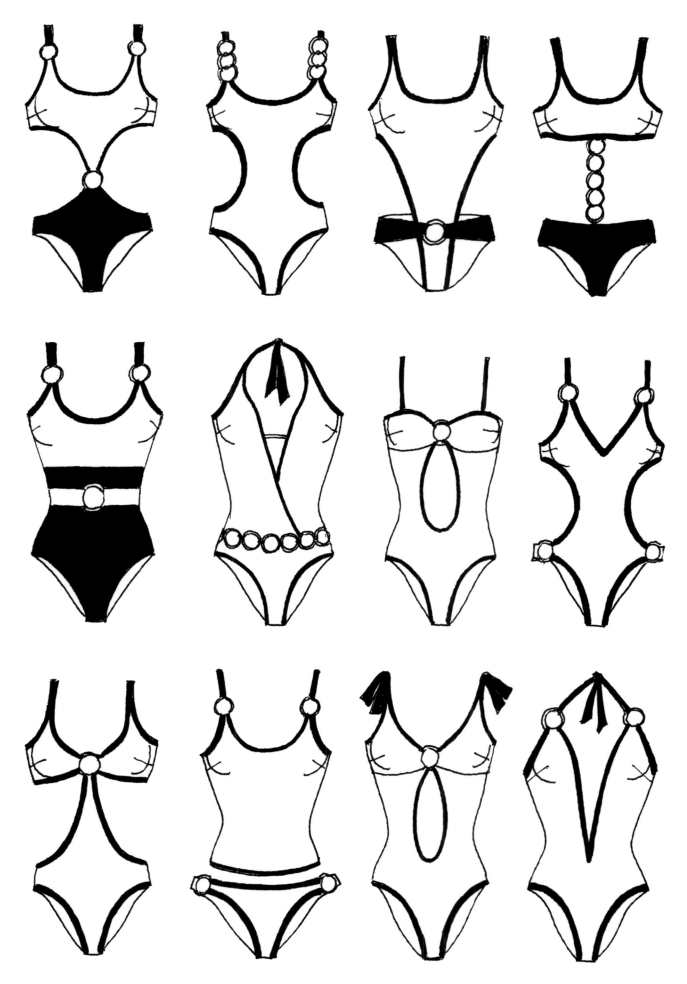

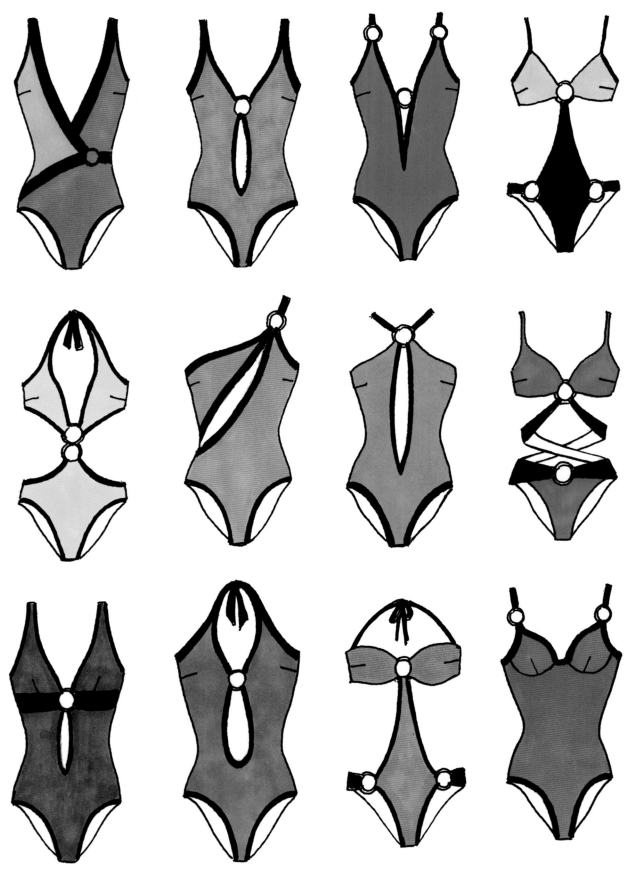

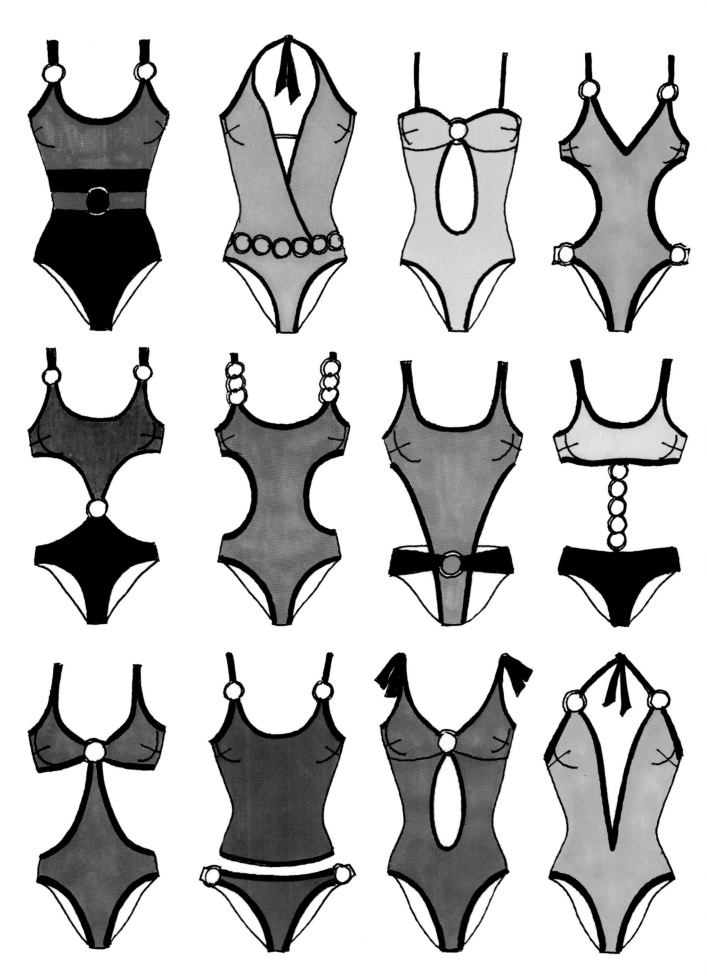

Bikinis with rings.

One-piece swimsuit
with rings.

Bikini with rings, underwire
and bust cups.

Unstructured bikini with rings and drawstring on both top and slip.

Bikini with rings on both bandeau top and briefs.

Triangle bikini with internal padding, rings on the top and briefs.

Elongated unpadded triangle bikini laced at the neck. Rings on top and briefs.

Trikini with rings.

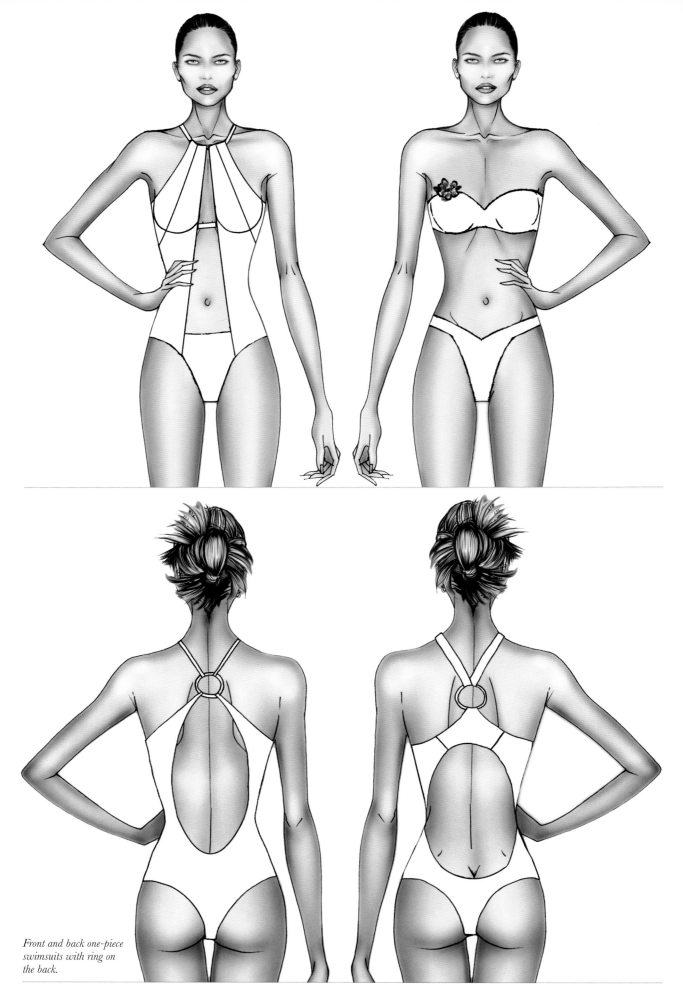

Front and back one-piece swimsuits with ring on the back.

Gold laminated one-piece swimsuit.

*Vichy jacquard Lycra with
thermo-welded raw cut edgings.*

163

*Trikini with rings and voile
kaftan with drawstring on
the shoulders.*

*Wet-look lycra Trikini (high shine)
with matt lycra straps.*

*Optical print polka dot trikini
with rings.*

One-piece swimsuit
with side rings.

Bikini with internal underwire
and lining with silver micro
stud decoration on floral print.

Mini printed stretch viscose
jersey beach dress.

Elongated triangle bikini and side ring with rhinestones.

Printed trikini with stirrup-shaped rings.

Back of printed one-piece swimsuit with rings.

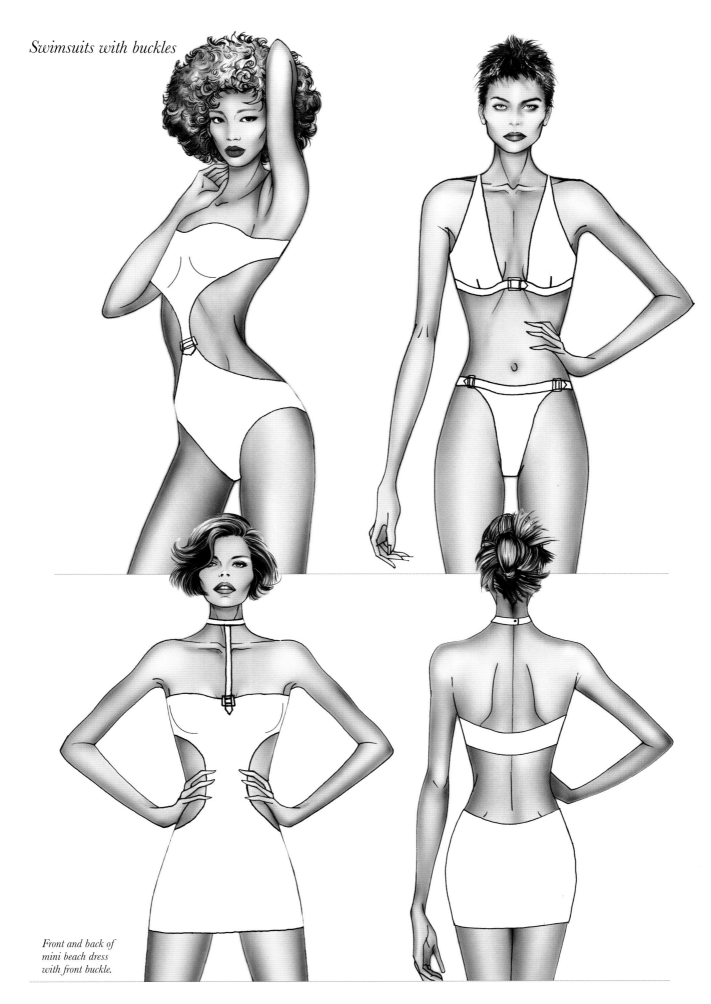

Swimsuits with buckles

*Front and back of
mini beach dress
with front buckle.*

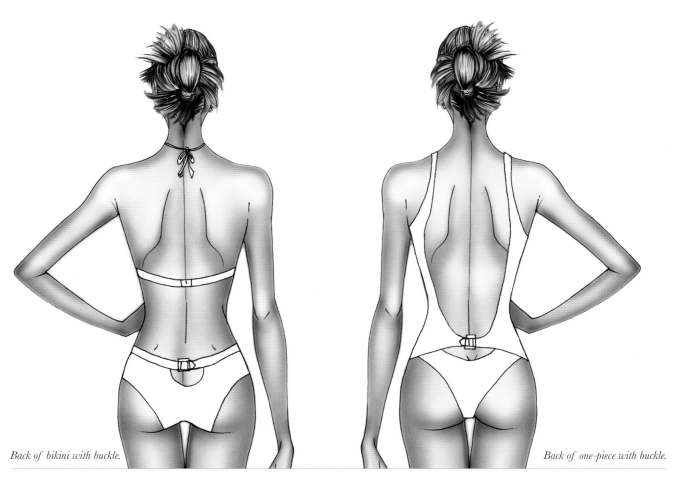

Back of bikini with buckle.

Back of one-piece with buckle.

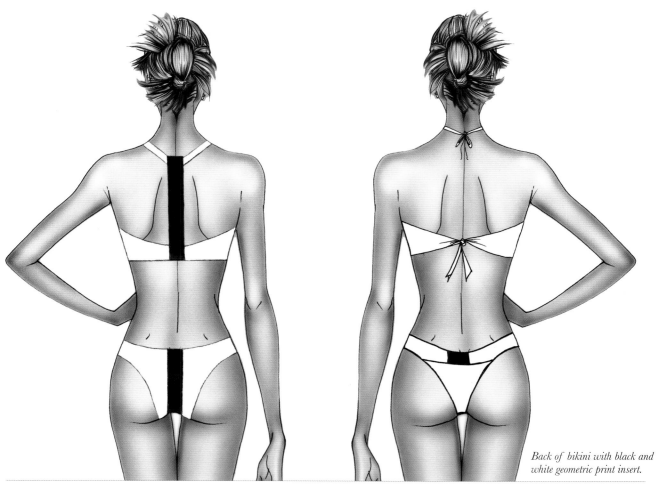

Back of bikini with black and white geometric print insert.

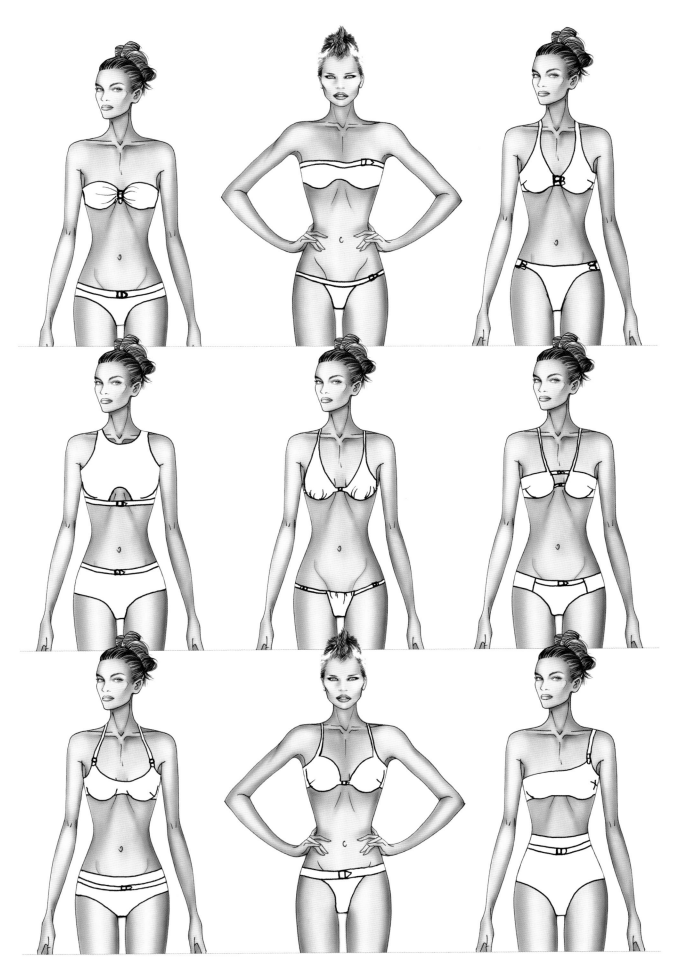

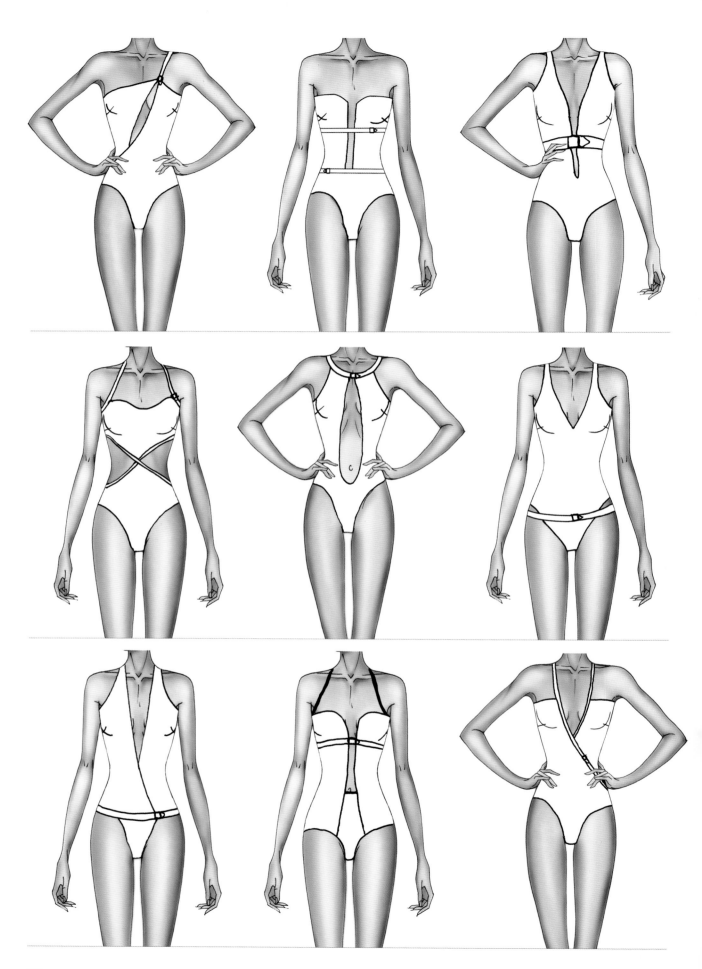

Bikini with accessories with buckle.

Trikini with black and white geometric print inserts.

*Strapless swimsuit with underwire and inner
cups at the bust. Geometric print inserts.*

*Front and back of mini beach
dress with black and white
geometric print inserts.*

*Unstructured bust bikini
with laces on the briefs.*

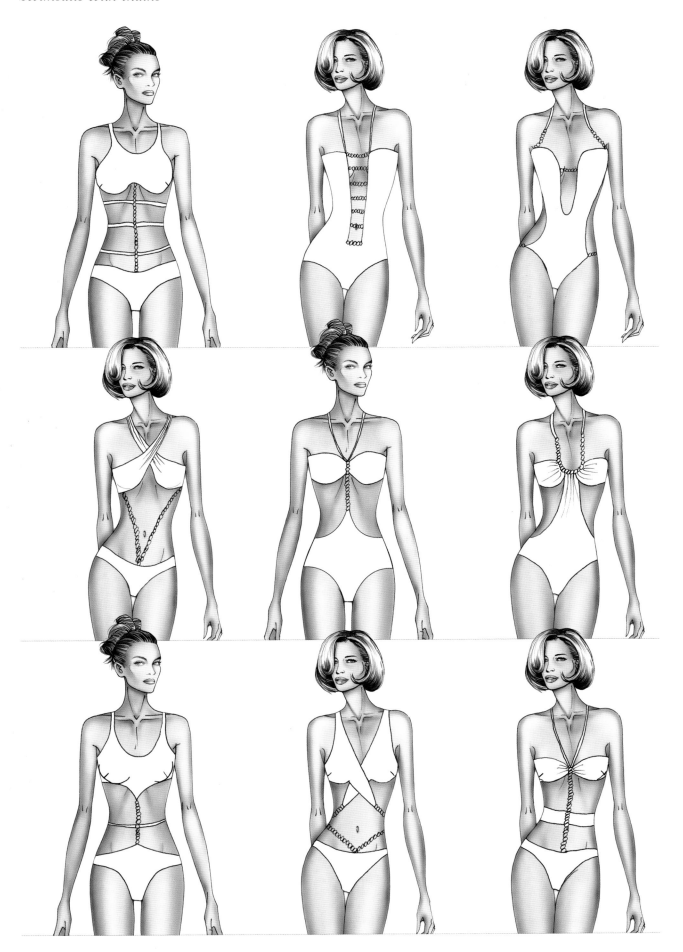

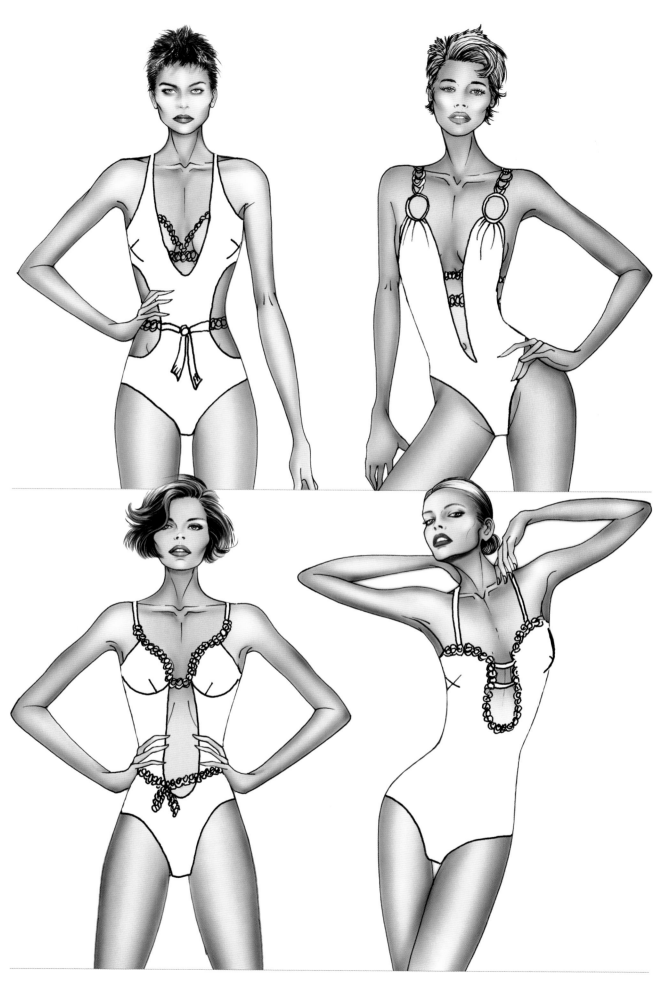

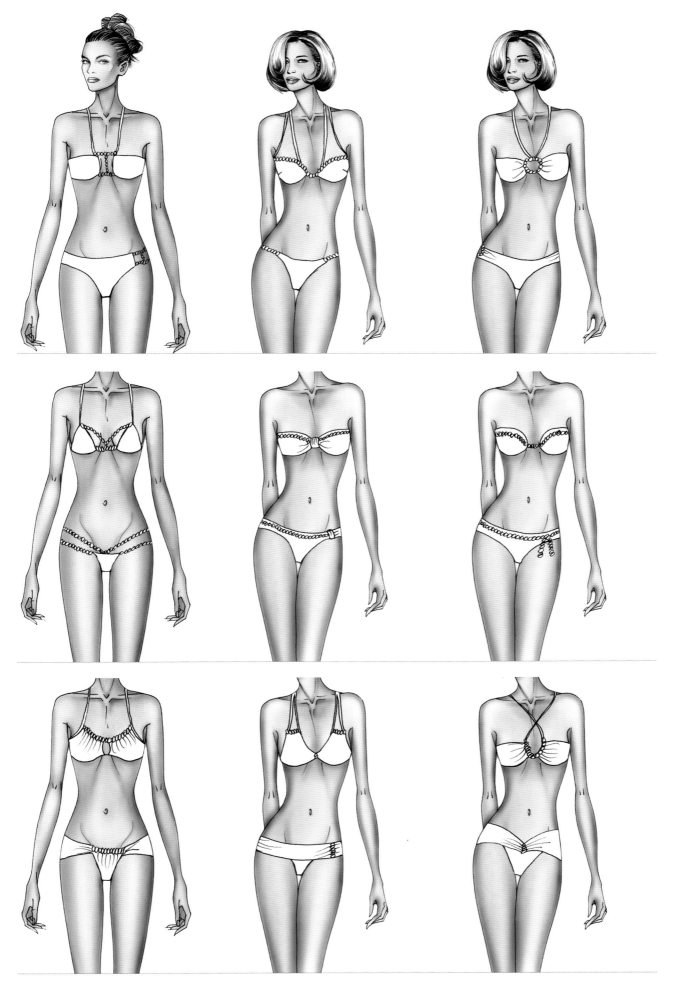

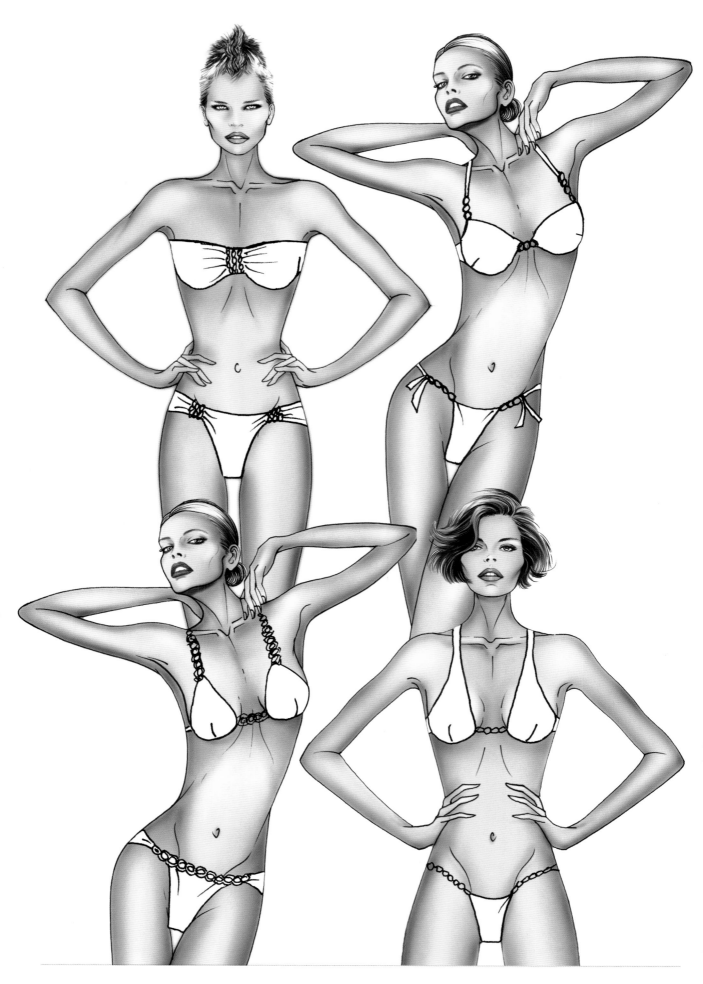

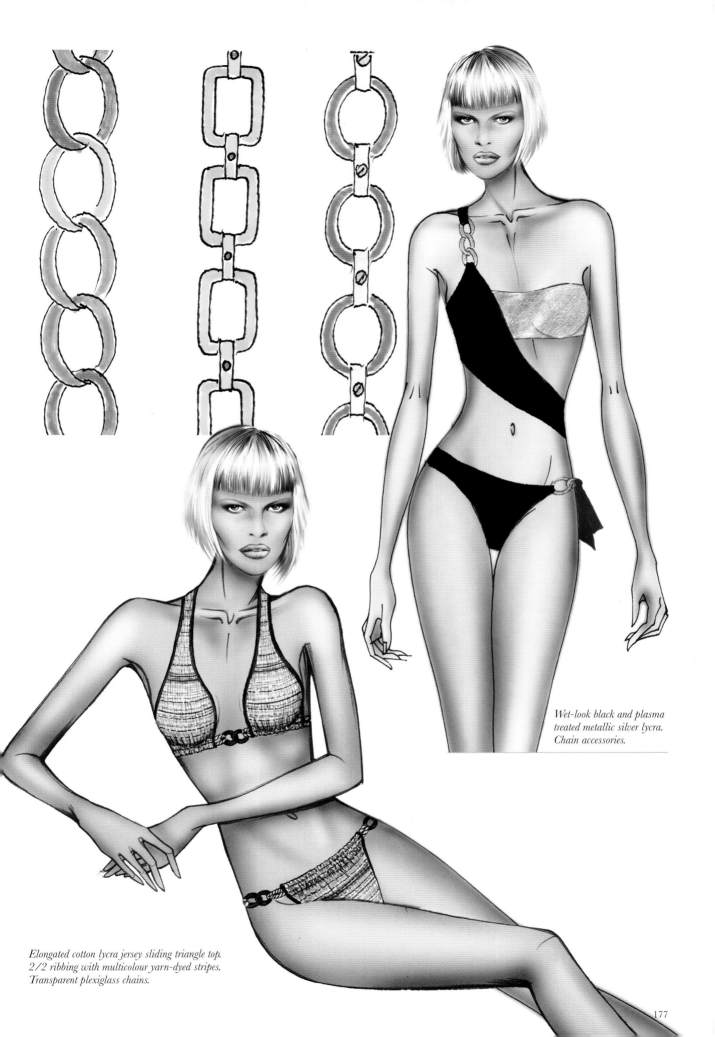

Wet-look black and plasma treated metallic silver lycra. Chain accessories.

Elongated cotton lycra jersey sliding triangle top. 2/2 ribbing with multicolour yarn-dyed stripes. Transparent plexiglass chains.

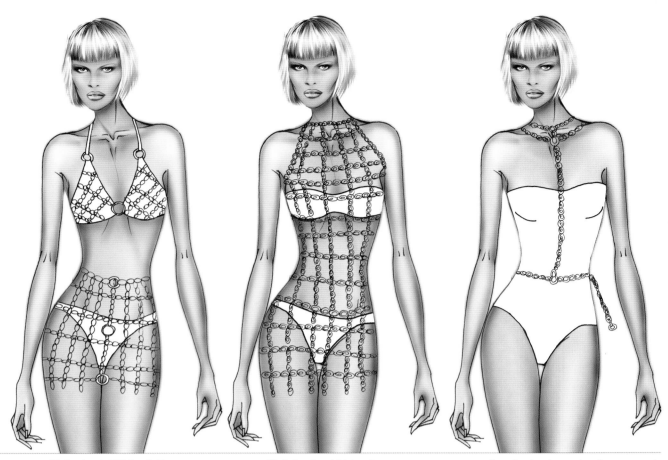

Chain triangle bikini and skirt.

Chain bandeau bikini and mini dress.

One-piece bandeau swimsuit with chain accessory.

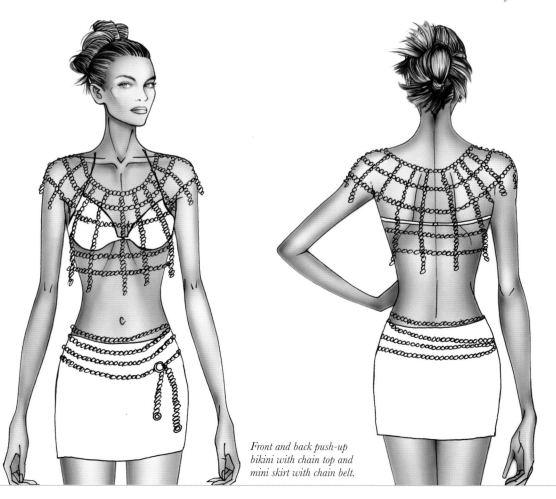

Front and back push-up bikini with chain top and mini skirt with chain belt.

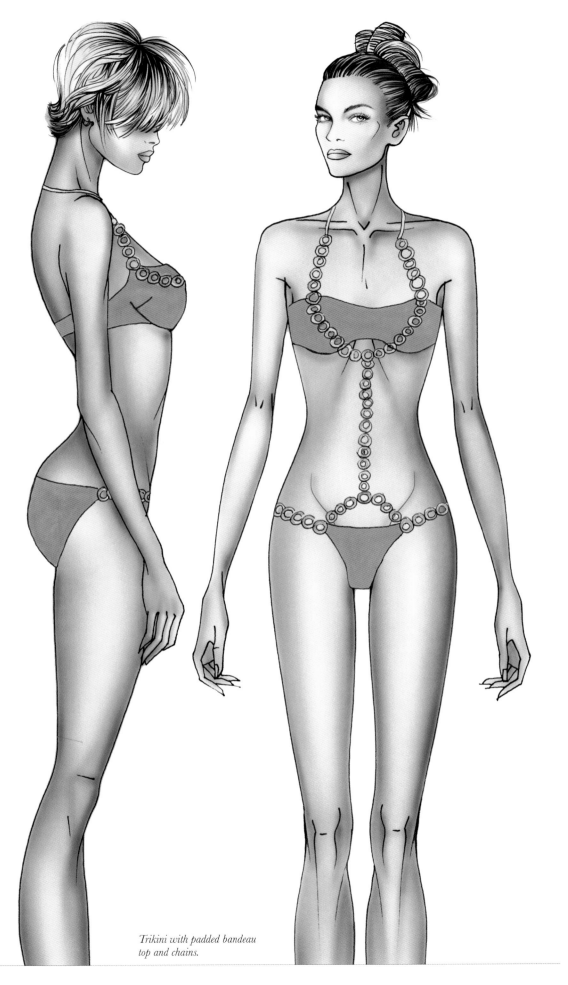

*Trikini with padded bandeau
top and chains.*

Bikinis and trikinis with multicoloured inserts

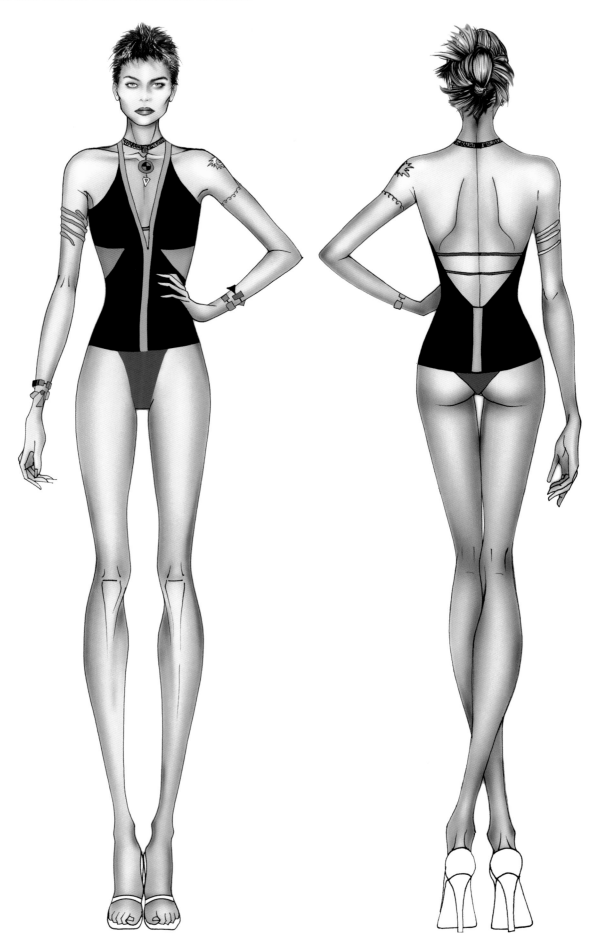

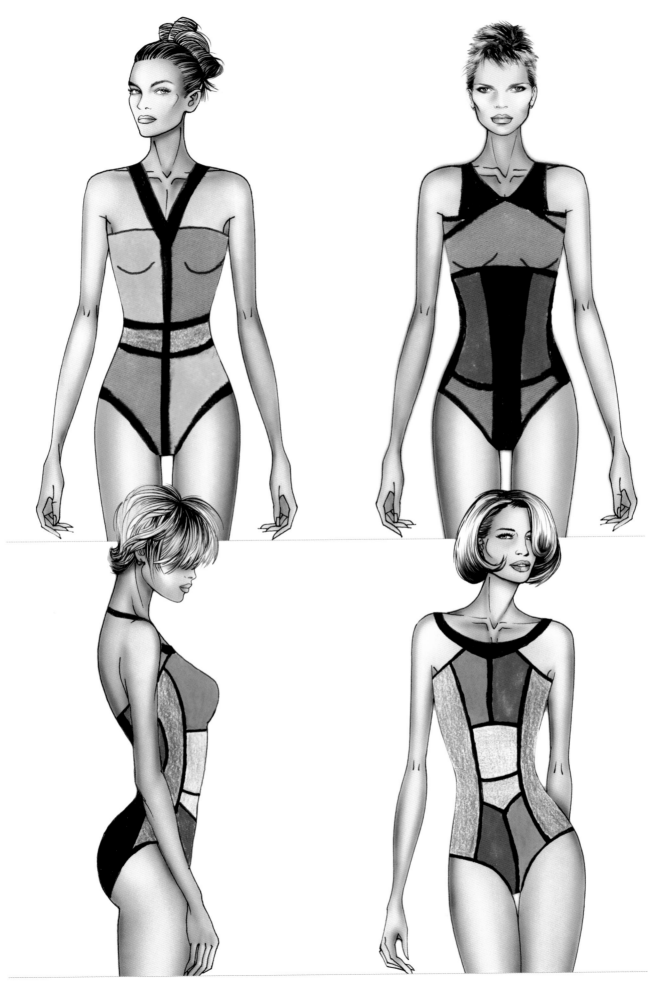

Sport inspired

Laser-cut tracery and raw cut edges. Lined with contrasting mesh and metallic decoration.

One-piece swimsuit with heat-sealed transparent and coloured PVC inserts and metallised laminae.

Laser-cut inlays and raw cut decoration

Laser-cut traceries with coloured lining

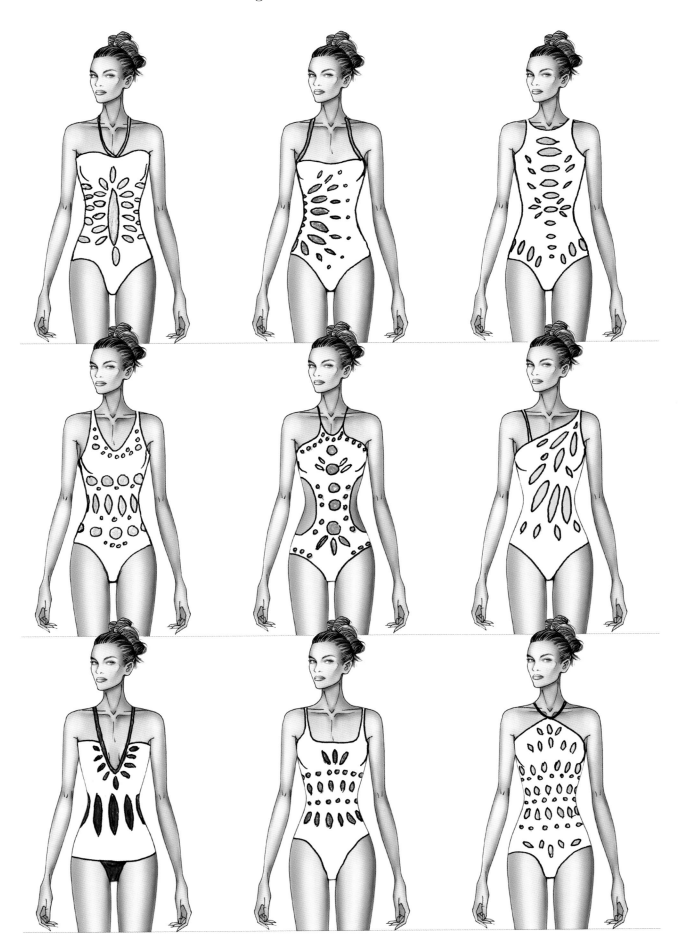

Laser-cut traceries. White background with black lining underneath.

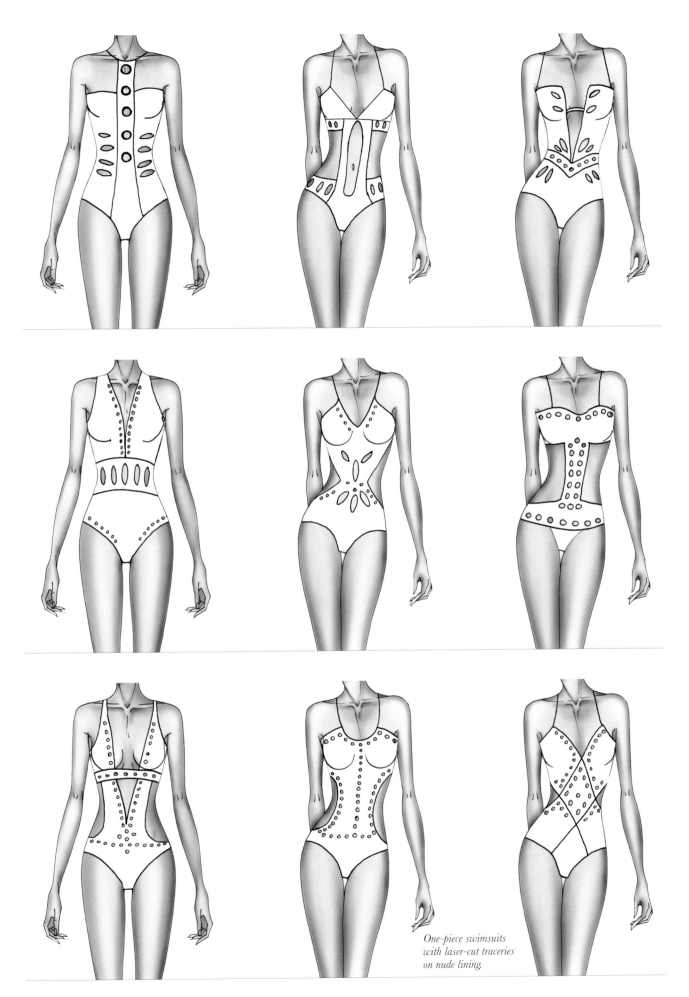

*One-piece swimsuits
with laser-cut traceries
on nude lining.*

Laser-cut stretch fabric.
Black lining.

Front and back of a laser-cut
swimsuit with a contrasting
turquoise lining.

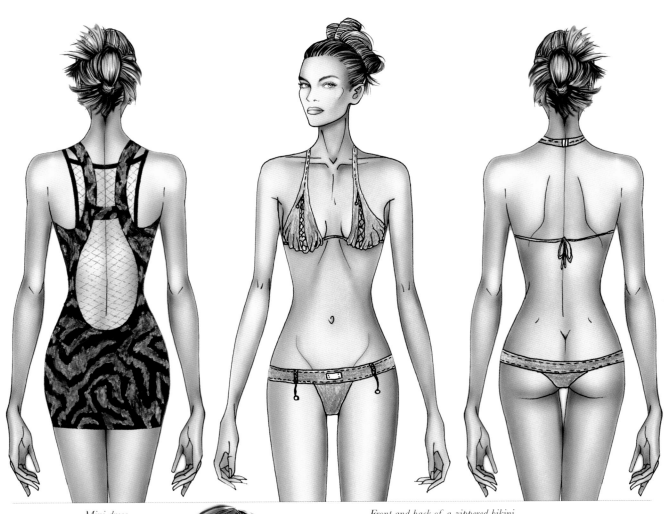

Mini dress.

Front and back of a zippered bikini.

Top and shorts.

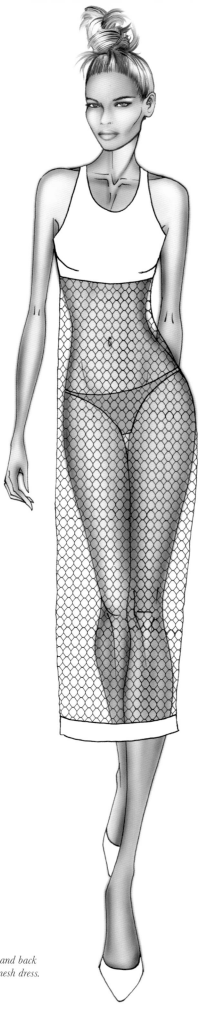

*Front and back
of a mesh dress.*

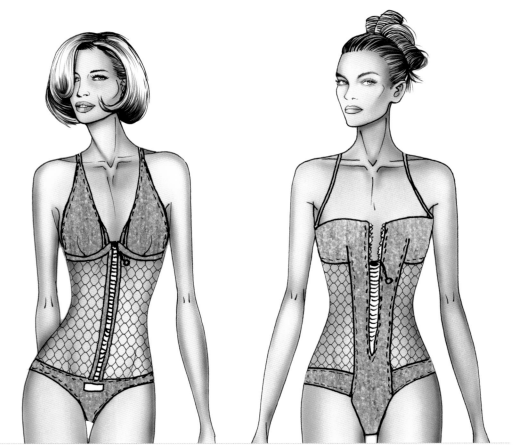

*One-piece swimsuits
with zips and mesh.*

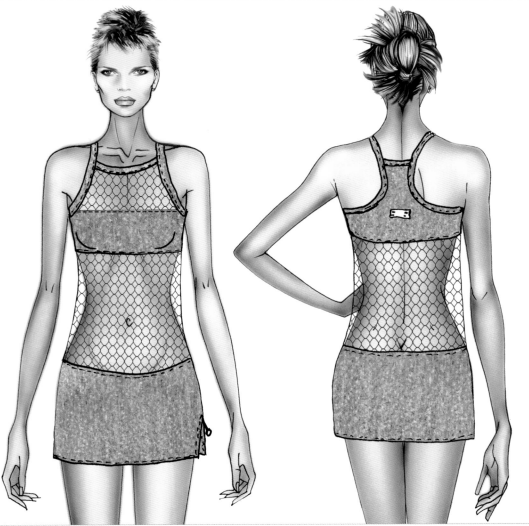

*Front and back of a
mini dress with mesh.*

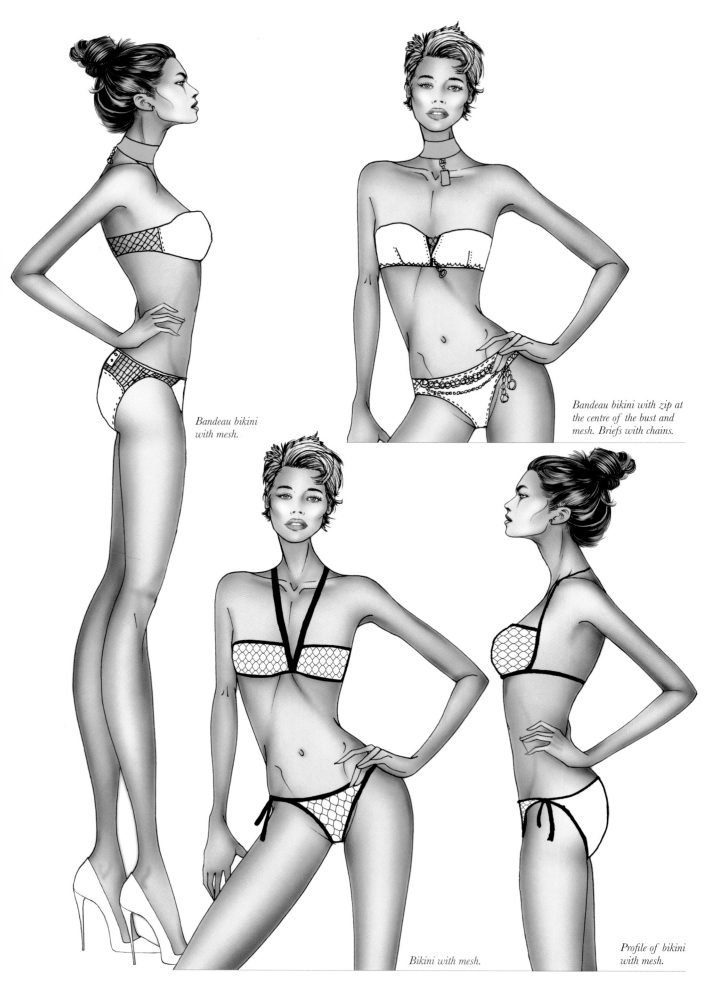

Bandeau bikini with mesh.

Bandeau bikini with zip at the centre of the bust and mesh. Briefs with chains.

Bikini with mesh.

Profile of bikini with mesh.

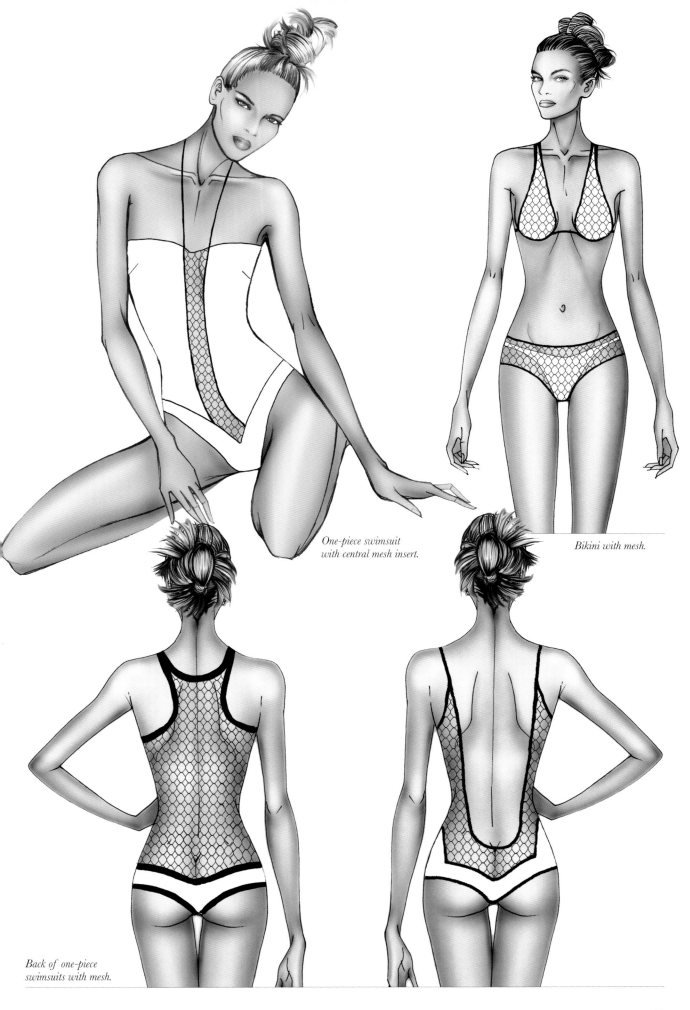

*One-piece swimsuit
with central mesh insert.*

Bikini with mesh.

*Back of one-piece
swimsuits with mesh.*

*Front and back of
one-piece swimsuit
with zip.*

*Front and back of
swimsuit with mesh.*

*Front and back of
mesh vest.*

One-piece swimsuit
with shaded print,
mesh insert and zip.

Tapered cotton terry mini bathrobe.
Inside pockets on the sides.
Reflective straps with logos along
the sleeves. Various embroideries on
labels and neck.

Floral print bikini with silver laminated inserts and contrasting edging.

Short summer dressing gown in light jacquard terry with 2/2 ribbing and mesh inserts. Inside pockets on the sides.

Ethnic Inspired

Crossed two-tone faux leather straps with studs.

Printed one-piece swimsuit with sarong and macramé shoulder motif.

Central plastron in three-colour macramé. Stretch faux leather straps.

Long two-print beach dress with necklace effect accessory.

Faux leather straps with tribal embroidery and print. Antique silver accessories.

Top with high-waist trousers.

Faux leather stretch strap trikini with antique silver and turquoise accessories.

Long printed beach dress. Metal accessory shoulder straps and leather straps.

Bikini with bandeau top with faux leather straps. Accessories with turquoise stones.

Mini two-print beach dress.

Bikini with embroidered top and faux leather braids. Striped printed briefs.

Two-print top and sarong skirt.

Sarong dress.

Bust print trikini with necklace effect multicolour bead decoration and mini macramé sarong.

Printed one-piece swimsuit with printed stretch faux leather belt.

Bikini with crossed stretch faux leather straps. Nude lining only on the bust.

Convertible one-piece swimsuit with adjustable bands: by pulling out the three central ones, it becomes a bikini.

*Front and back of a bikini embroidered
with contrasting faux leather straps. Faux
leather shoulder straps and belt the colour
of the embroidery and faux ivory beads.*

Plain top and printed trouser skirt.

*Mini two-print beach dress with
necklace effect accessories.*

*Long two-colour beach dress with
macramé embroidery in the centre.*

Back of one-piece swimsuit with faux leather shoulder strap motif and central embroidery.

Small faux leather bolero embroidered with contrasting straps. Denim miniskirt.

Back of one-piece swimsuit with faux leather strap embroidery.

One-piece bandeau swimsuit with faux leather shoulder straps and embroidery, and faux ivory beads.

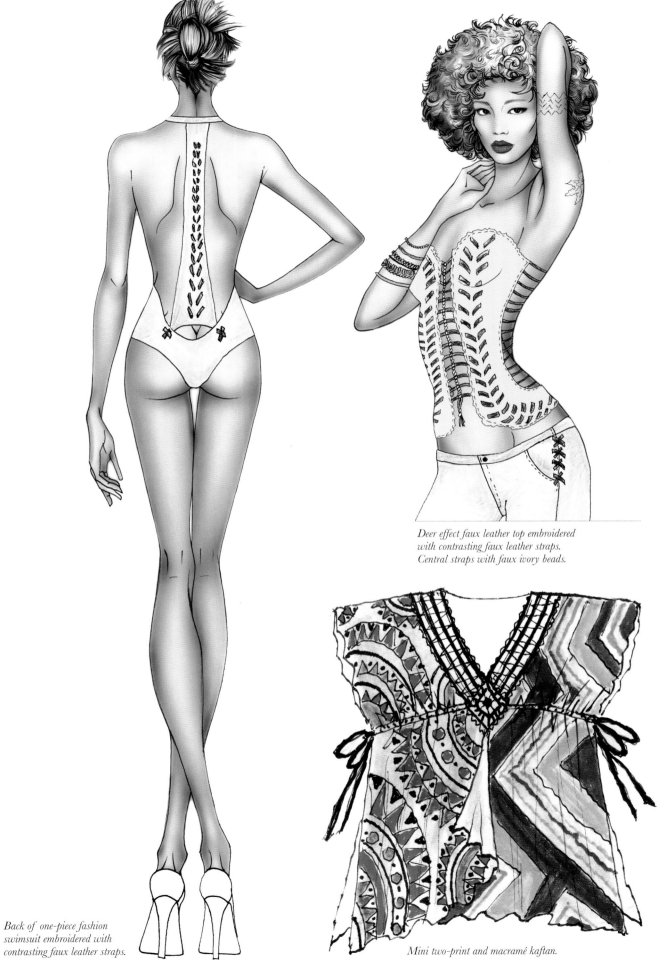

*Deer effect faux leather top embroidered
with contrasting faux leather straps.
Central straps with faux ivory beads.*

*Back of one-piece fashion
swimsuit embroidered with
contrasting faux leather straps.*

Mini two-print and macramé kaftan.

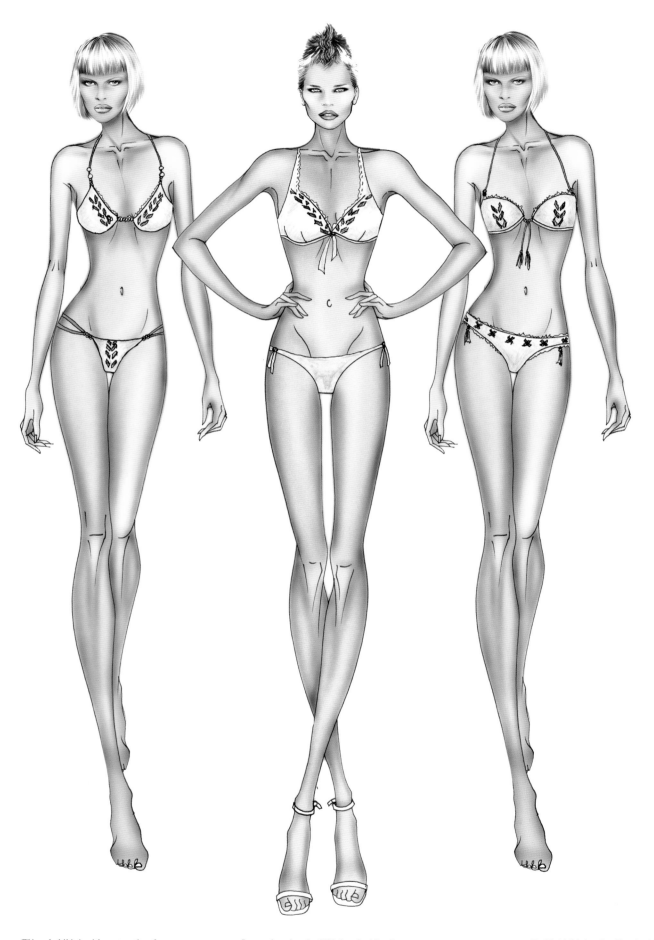

Triangle bikini with contrasting faux leather straps and faux ivory beads.

Internal underwire bikini embroidered with contrasting faux leather straps.

Padded bikini embroidered with contrasting faux leather straps.

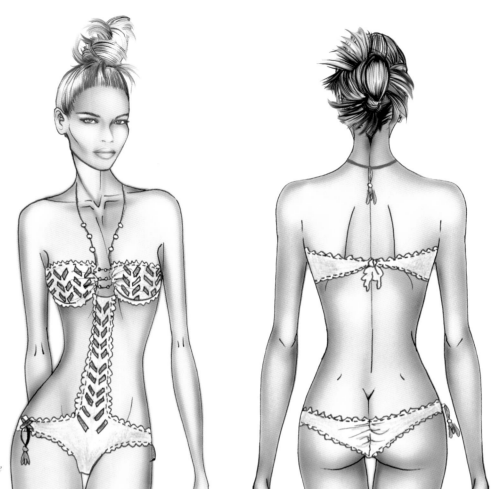

Front and back of an underwired padded trikini embroidered with contrasting faux leather straps and faux ivory beads at the centre of the bust and on the neck strap.

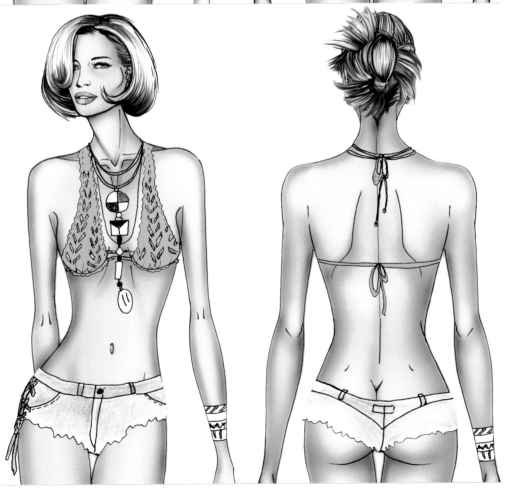

Front and back of a faux leather bikini embroidered with contrasting straps. Denim mini shorts embroidered with faux leather straps on the side.

Front and back of a one-piece swimsuit with faux leather strings at the centre and contrasting embroidery on the sides.

Shaded print one-piece swimsuit with faux leather straps in the centre of the bust, on the side and on the side of the briefs.

Tropical Inspired

Animalier print trikini with laser-cut flower decoration and beads.

One-piece swimsuit with laser-cut flower decoration and embroidery with small rhinestones on petals.

Triangle bikini with laser-cut flower decoration and synthetic raffia fringes.

Voile kaftan with laser-cut flower decoration and fringes.

One-piece bandeau swimsuit with macramé-effect embroidery, laser-cut flower decorations with beads and small rhinestones.

Sliding triangle bikini and tan mini shorts in deer-effect faux leather printed on the finished garment.

Printed sarong and top.

One-piece swimsuit with two animal prints.

One-piece swimsuits with laser-cut
flower decoration.

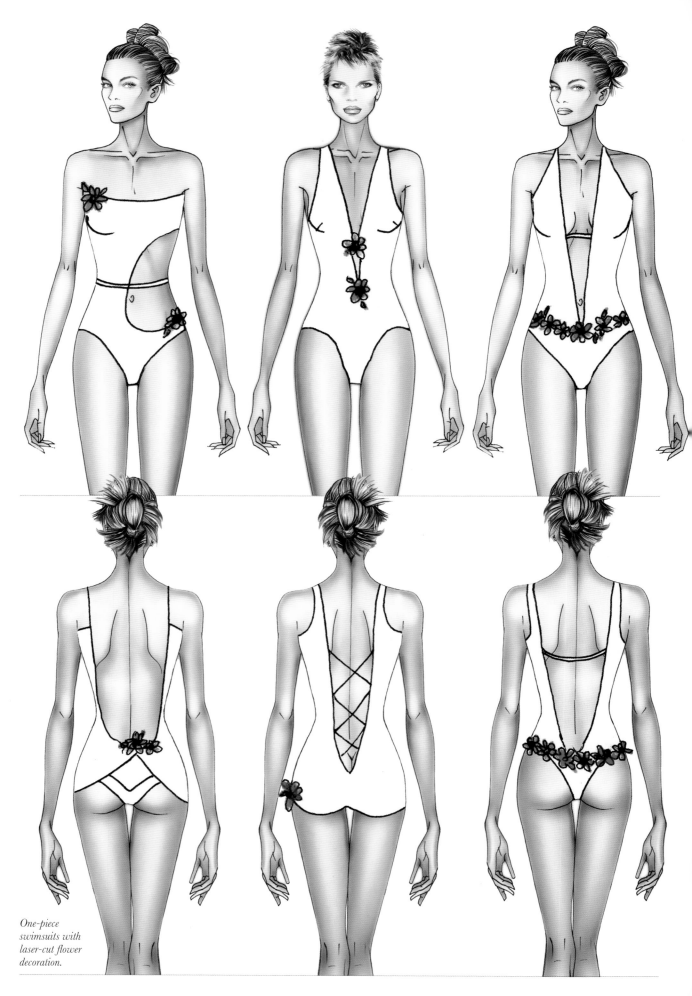

One-piece swimsuits with laser-cut flower decoration.

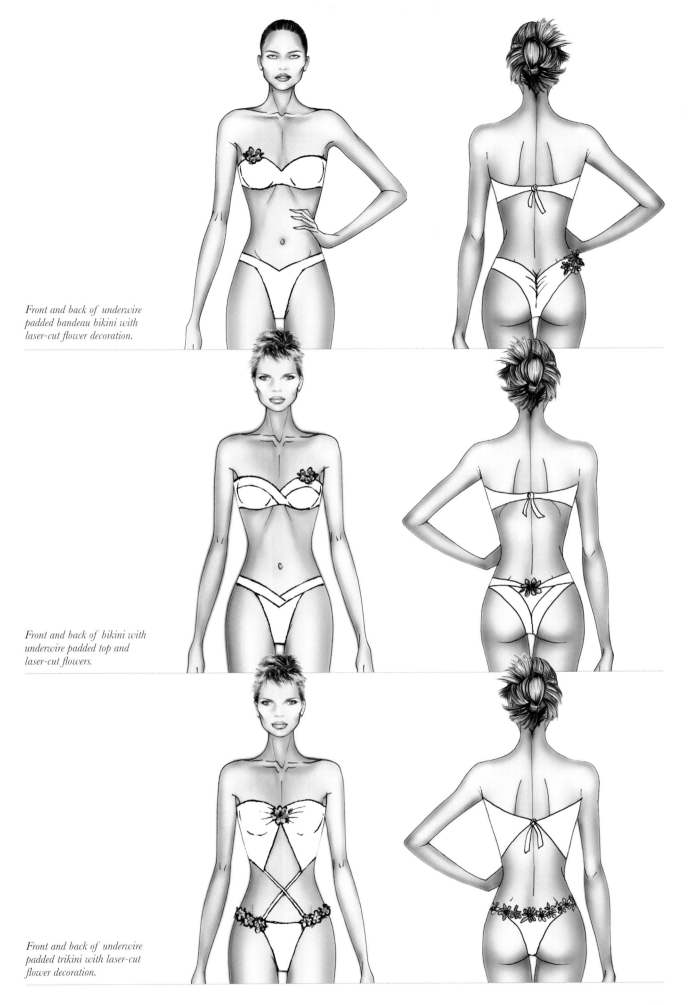

Front and back of underwire padded bandeau bikini with laser-cut flower decoration.

Front and back of bikini with underwire padded top and laser-cut flowers.

Front and back of underwire padded trikini with laser-cut flower decoration.

Floral motif.

Jungle all over.

Floral motif.

Animalier all over.

One colour floral design.

Animalier with flowers.

Floral all over.

Diagonal lines.

Madras and maxi polka dots.

Printed bikini with flower and small rhinestone decoration.

Bikini with laser-cut flower embroidery and bead embroidery.

Plain bikini with multicolour flower decoration.

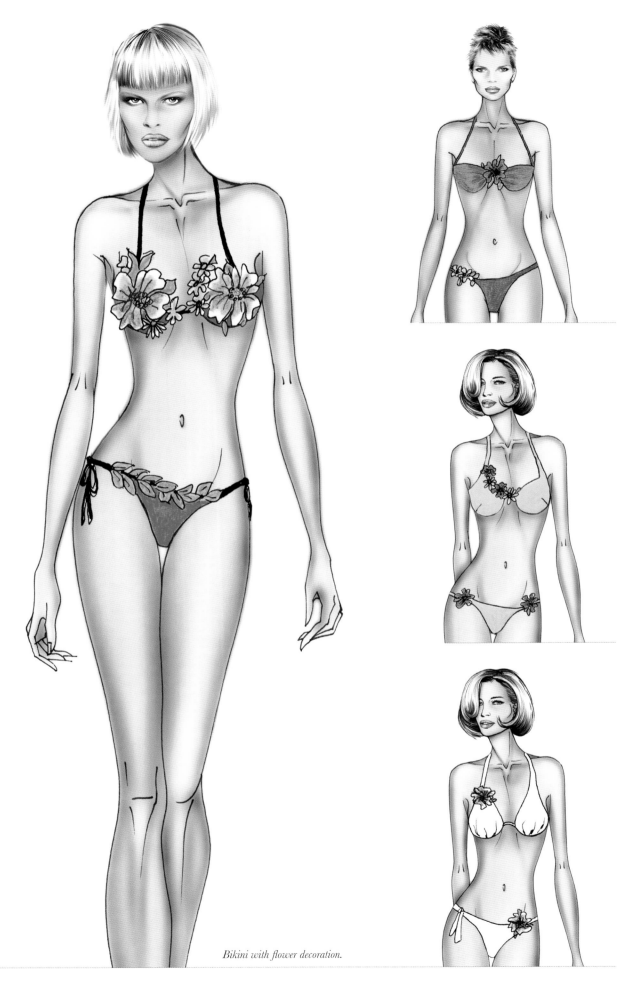

Bikini with flower decoration.

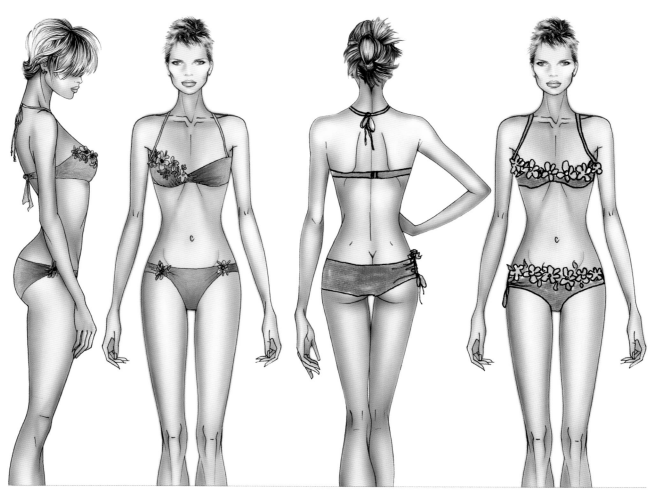

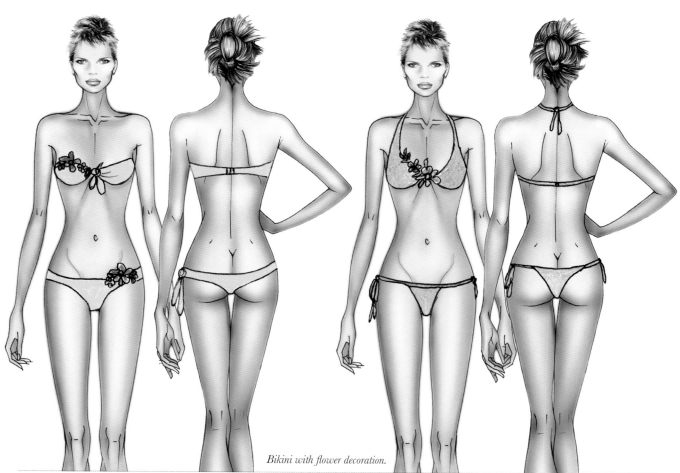

Bikini with flower decoration.

Mini beach dress with flower at centre bust and long fringes.

Front and back of top with flower decoration and fringes. Mini sarong with fringes.

Longuette beach dress with underbust flowers and many different multicolour fringes.

Printed beach dress with flower decoration and fringes.

Front and back of short printed kaftan with flower decoration on the neckline.

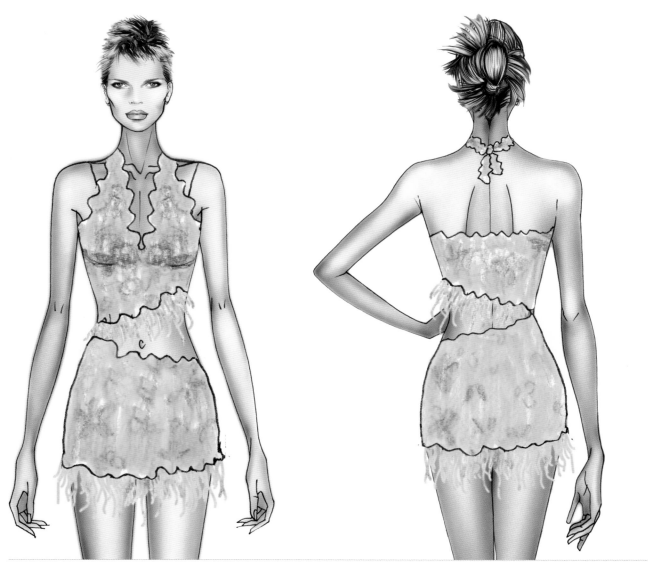

*Front and back of a
mini dress with fringes.*

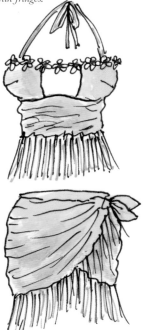

*Top with flower decoration and
fringes. Mini skirt with fringes.*

Sarong mini dress with fringes.

Top and shorts with fringes.

Front and back of one-piece swimsuit with flower decoration and fringes.

Printed trikini with mini sarong.

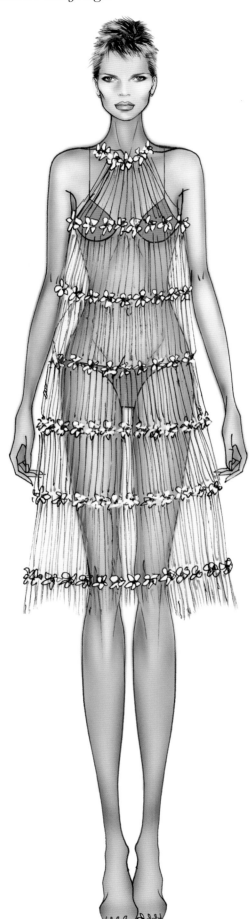

*Front and back of
beach dress.*

Front and back of one-piece swimsuits.

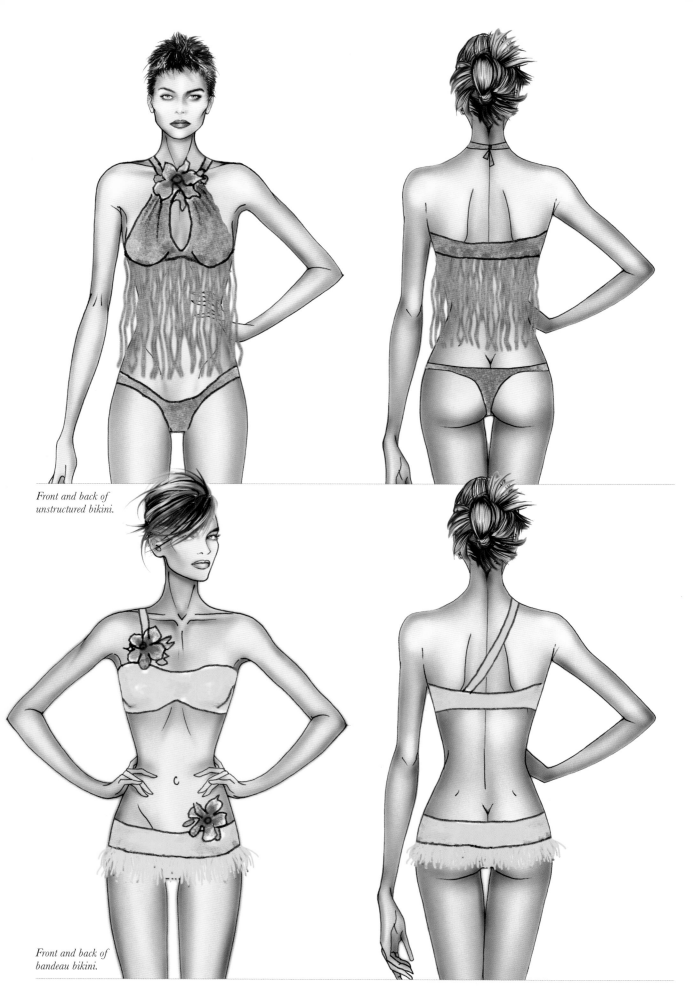

*Front and back of
unstructured bikini.*

*Front and back of
bandeau bikini.*

Matt lycra tankini with print and plain briefs.

*Printed tankini with laser-cut flower decoration,
beads in the centre and fringes.*

Printed bikini with flower embroidery decoration.

One-piece swimsuit with
antique gold laminated print
and screen printing. Embroidery
on the bust band.

Print top and camouflage
print shorts.

Matt lycra bandeau bikini with zip.
Camouflage print and detachable
shoulder straps in stretch faux leather
like the trim of the briefs.

Jungle print trikini with animalier print shoulder strap.

Drawstring adjustable bandeau bikini and briefs. Metallic effect plasma treated camouflage print. Stretch faux leather strings.

Canvas waistcoat with camouflage print. Leggings with tiger print. Foulard tied at the waist. Matt lycra bikini with jungle floral print.

Long chenille jacquard dressing gown with hood and drawstring at the waist. Zip fastening. Internal side pockets. Hood and inside lined with fuchsia terry.

Garment dyed crocheted tankini.

Printed bikini with floral and madras motifs.

Elongated sliding triangle top with embroidery and beads on stretch tulle background. White lycra lining.

Ribbed jersey and lace top. Long patchwork print skirt in cotton muslin and different laces.

Bandeau top with small inner side slat. Doll stitch and lace trim.

*Dévoré jacquard polyamide lycra
one-piece swimsuit with nude lining.
Velvet effect areas alternating with
transparent areas.*

*Crochet-finish bandeau bikini
and mesh effect crocheted top
with beads and fringes.*

Sliding triangle bikini with multicolour honeycomb embroidery (or smock stitch).

Stretch trim central section with beads or sequins.

Crochet mesh jumpsuit with fringes. Triangle bikini.

Printed cotton fabric long shirt with a mix of embroideries. Printed stretch cotton jersey leggings.

*Wet-look lycra trikini
with polka dot print
and long fringes.*

*Raw cut unstructured triangle
bikini with zig - zag finish.
Embroidery with micro sequins
and multicolour beads.*

*Printed voile beach dress with
drawstring fringes at the waist.*

*Long patchwork print cotton voile
kaftan. Giant braid trim and
satin ribbons.*

*Beach dress in printed cotton gauze
and different macramé laces.*

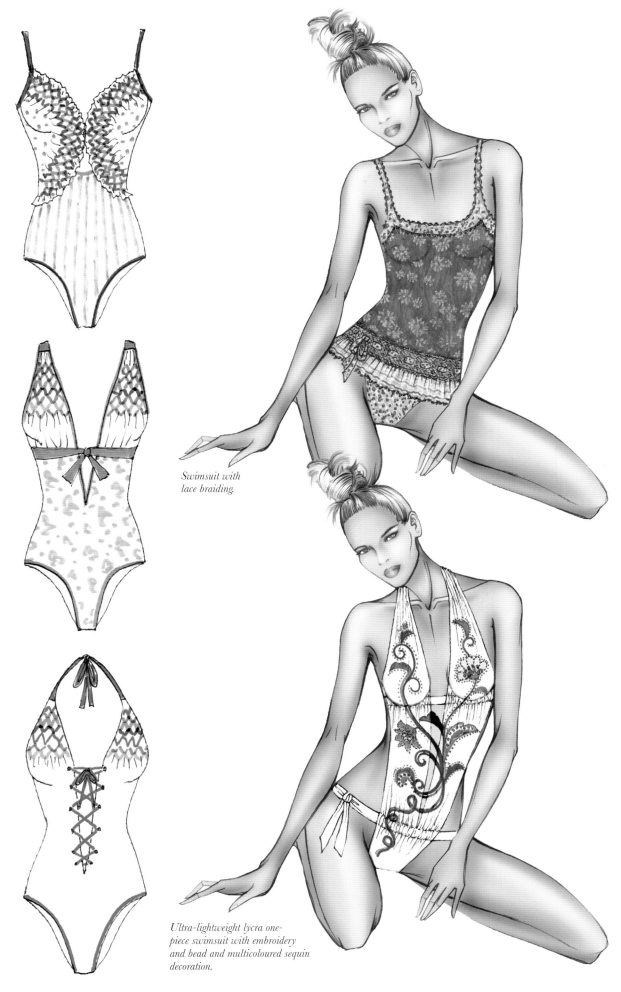

Swimsuit with lace braiding.

Ultra-lightweight lycra one-piece swimsuit with embroidery and bead and multicoloured sequin decoration.

Side view of an adjustable bandeau top with drawstring. Lycra fabric with all over multicolour embroidery.

Printed bikini with macramé lurex decoration.

Patchwork print bikini with micro designs. Accessory with necklace effect multicolour gemstones.

One-piece swimsuit with crocheted rings, faux leather trim with embroidery and beads embroidered in the centre.

Push-up bikini with coloured faux leather, macramé and beaded straps.

Brasil

Top and skirt with lace
flounces and print on the
finished garment.

Bikini with print on
the finished garment.
Volans lace flounces.

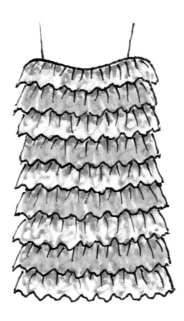

Triangle bikini with ruffles on the neckline and briefs with laces at the hips.

Bikini with ruffles on the padded top and on the sides of the briefs.

Trikini with ruffles.

*Front and back of one-piece swimsuit with
underwire and inner cups. Lacing on the
neck and deep neckline with ruffles.*

*Bandeau one-piece swimsuits with ruffles
at the neckline and where the briefs attach.*

*Ruffles of multicolour
ribbons and small
rhinestones.*

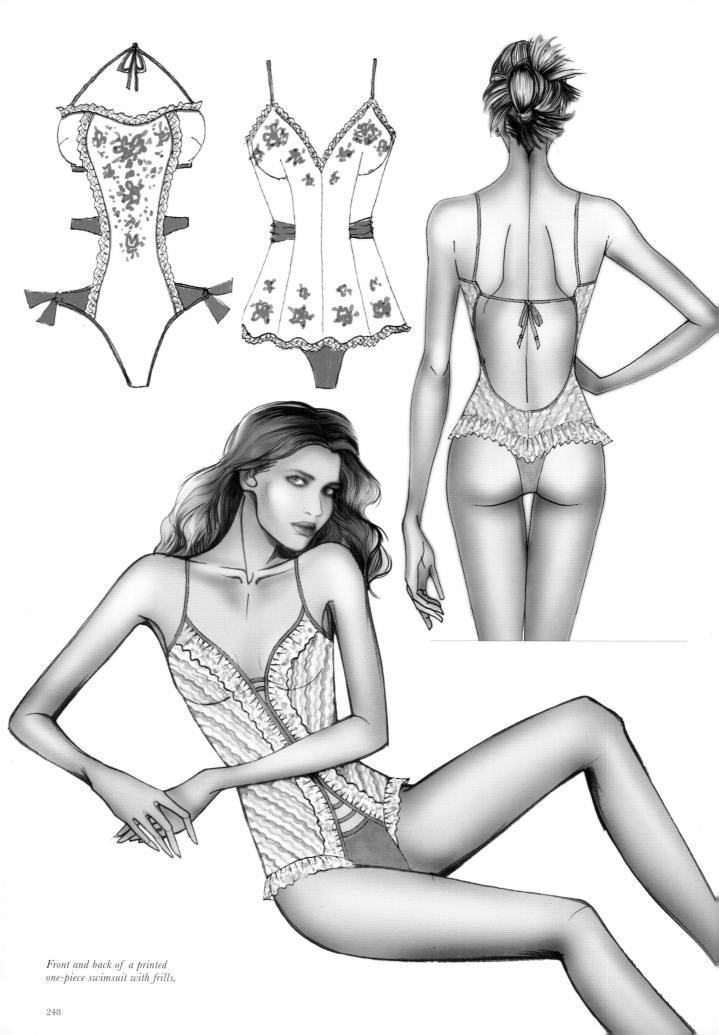

*Front and back of a printed
one-piece swimsuit with frills.*

Front and back of bikini with sliding triangle (with drawstring) and ruffles. Lace-up briefs.

Bikini with stretch tulle top and multicolour bead embroidery. Briefs with contrasting lining and double tulle frills.

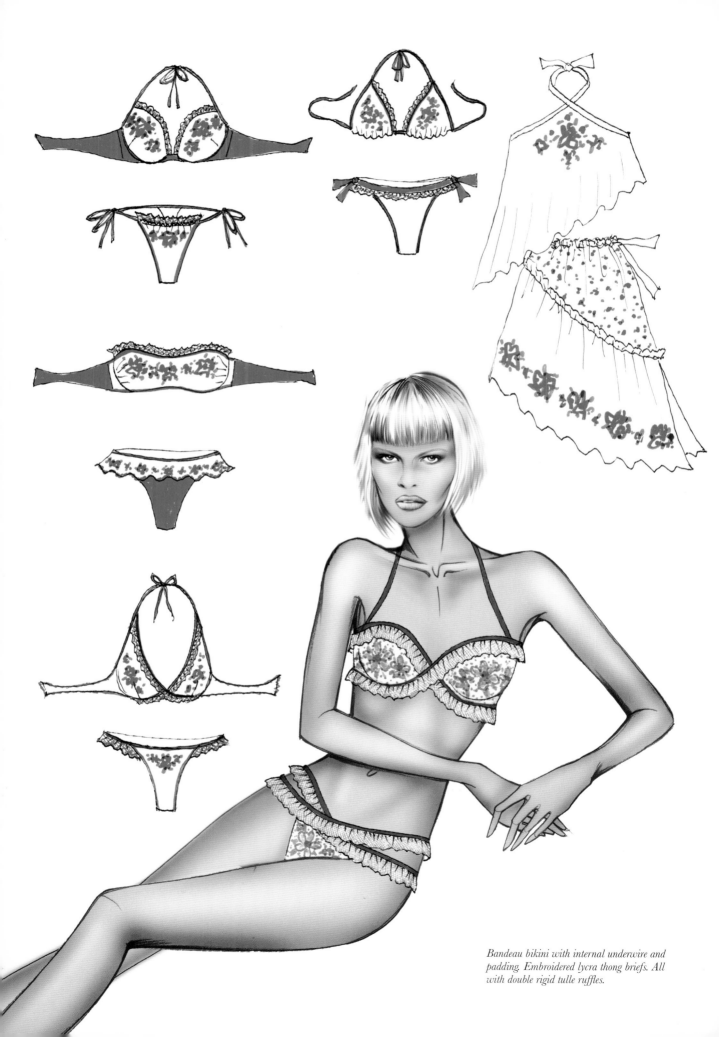

Bandeau bikini with internal underwire and padding. Embroidered lycra thong briefs. All with double rigid tulle ruffles.

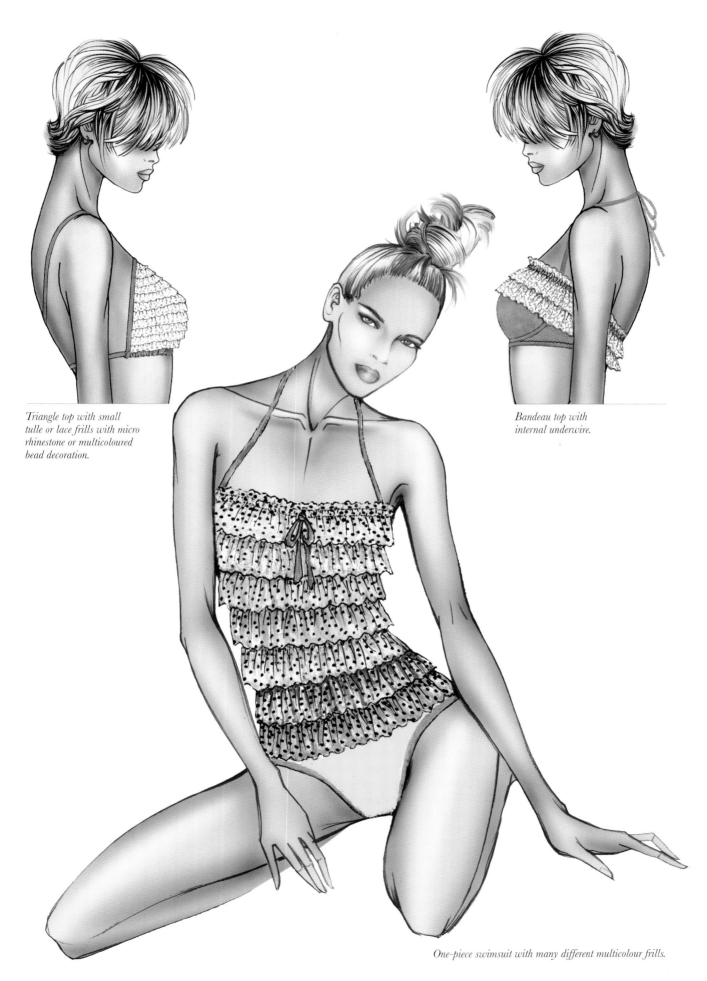

Triangle top with small tulle or lace frills with micro rhinestone or multicoloured bead decoration.

Bandeau top with internal underwire.

One-piece swimsuit with many different multicolour frills.

251

Dorina Croci began her professional training with a baccalaureate from the Istituto Tecnico Femminile Santa Caterina Da Siena in Milan.

After a period of study in the Faculty of Literature and Foreign Languages, given her natural propensity for drawing and her passion for art and costume, Dorina decided to devote herself to fashion and to take up the profession of designer.

She launched her career in the world of Underwear and Beachwear, an inspiring and stimulating sector that has given her the opportunity to work as a freelancer with leading Italian and foreign fashion houses: Triumph, Parah, Fiorucci, Olmo, Harno, Jantzen, Schiesser, Paloma Picasso, Imec, Franca Von Wunster and many others.

In addition, her most recent collaborations include the design of a Trend Book for the fashion shows of Paris, and the creation of a collection of drawings for handmade fabrics for the Cannes Fair.

Dorina is now one of the most successful and creative designers of underwear and beachwear, and with this book she has decided to share her decades of experience. This new project is meant to be, in fact, a source of inspiration, help and support to stimulate the imagination of fans, students and those working in the world of Beachwear and Underwear Fashion Design.

The many brand new designs on these pages display the infinite variety of models, fabrics and patterns possible. What is more, Dorina hired Elisabetta "Kuky" Drudi, renowned for her drawings of the human figure, to illustrate the book and make it look even more interesting and professional.

Elisabetta Drudi A graduate of the Istituto d'Arte F. Mengaroni in Pesaro, Elisabetta currently works with Italian and international companies as a designer and illustrator. Her five years of experience running her own business have led her to plan and manage fashion shows and collections for companies in Italy and Europe.

Alongside her mentor Tiziana Paci she is the author of the international bestsellers *Figure Drawing for Fashion Design* and *Figure Drawing for Men's Fashion*. Today, she works as a fashion and textile designer with prestigious international firms.

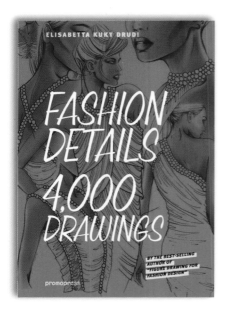

FASHION DETAILS
4,000 Drawings
Elisabetta Kuky Drudi

978-84-92810-95-6
195 x 285 mm. 384 pp.

This title by best-selling author Elisabetta Drudi is an inspirational sourcebook for drawing fashion details. Featuring four thousand original sketches, it contains everything you need to discover how to make accurate drawings of a wide range of fashion elements and is an invaluable resource for designers, illustrators, artists, students and anyone involved in fashion design.

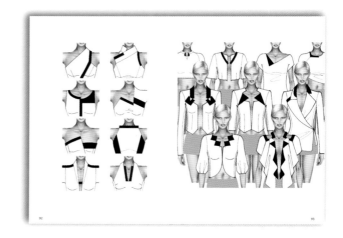

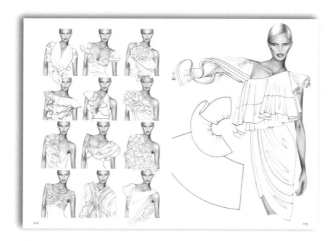

FASHION SKETCHING
Templates, Poses and Ideas for Fashion Design
Claudia Ausonia Palazio

978-84-16504-10-7
195 x 285 mm. 272 pp.

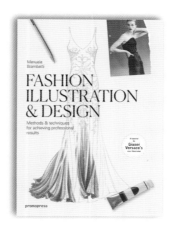

FASHION ILLUSTRATION & DESIGN
Methods & Techniques for Achieving Professional Results
Manuela Brambatti

978-84-16851-06-5
215 x 300 mm. 240 pp.

COLOUR IN FASHION ILLUSTRATION
Drawing and Painting Techniques
Tiziana Paci

978-84-16851-59-1
215 x 287 mm. 320 pp.

PRINTED TEXTILE DESIGN
Profession, Trends & Project Development
Marie-Christine Nöel
Michaël Cailloux

978-84-15967-67-5
215 x 280 mm. 192 pp.

COUTURE UNFOLDED
Pleats, Folds and Draping in Fashion Design
Brunella Giannangeli

978-84-16851-91-1
183 x 256 mm. 120 pp.

PALETTE PERFECT
Color Combinations Inspired by Fashion, Art & Style
Lauren Wager

978-84-15967-90-3
148 x 210 mm. 304 pp.